COURAGEOUS
TRAINING

COURAGEOUS TRAINING

Bold Actions for Business Results

Tim Mooney and
Robert O. Brinkerhoff

Berrett–Koehler Publishers, Inc.
San Francisco
a BK Business book

Berrett-Koehler Publishers, Inc.
235 Montgomery Street, Suite 650
San Francisco, CA 94104-2916
Tel: (415) 288-0260; Fax: (415) 362-2512 www.bkconnection.com

Ordering Information

Quantity sales Special discounts are available on quantity purchases by corporations, associations, and others. For details, contact the "Special Sales Department" at the Berrett-Koehler address above.

Individual sales Berrett-Koehler publications are available through most bookstores. They can also be ordered directly from Berrett-Koehler: Tel: (800) 929-2929; Fax: (802) 864-7626; www.bkconnection.com.

Orders for college textbook/course adoption use Please contact Berrett-Koehler: Tel: (800) 929-2929; Fax: (802) 864-7626.

Orders by U.S. trade bookstores and wholesalers Please contact Ingram Publisher Services, Tel: (800) 509-4887; Fax: (800) 838-1149; E-mail: customer.service@ingram publisherservices.com; or visit www.ingrampublisherservices.com/Ordering for details about electronic ordering.

Berrett-Koehler and the BK logo are registered trademarks of Berrett-Koehler Publishers, Inc.

Printed in the United States of America

Berrett-Koehler books are printed on long-lasting acid-free paper. When it is available, we choose paper that has been manufactured by environmentally responsible processes. These may include using trees grown in sustainable forests, incorporating recycled paper, minimizing chlorine in bleaching, or recycling the energy produced at the paper mill.

Library of Congress Cataloging-in-Publication Data

Mooney, Tim, 1955–
Courageous training : bold actions for business results / Tim Mooney & Robert
   O. Brinkerhoff.
p. cm.
ISBN 978-1-57675-564-8 (pbk. : alk. paper)
1. Employees—Training of.   I. Brinkerhoff, Robert O.   II. Title.

HF5549.5.T7M627 2008
658.3'124—dc22
200812251

First Edition
13 12 11 10 09 08   10 9 8 7 6 5 4 3 2 1

Advantage Way is a registered trademark of the Advantage Performance Group.

Tim Mooney dedicates this book to his parents, Joan and Ray, who inspired him to never settle for good enough and taught him that big dreams combined with clarity of belief and hard work will prevail in the long run. Their self-sacrifice and love for their children continue to be an inspiration to this day.

Rob Brinkerhoff dedicates this book to Jane and Richard Auld, who had the courage to live with and raise their daughter Stevie, to whom Rob is now married and whose feistiness and beauty live on in their three daughters. Thanks to Jane and Dick also for their wondrously generous and highly principled values—a continuing source of inspiration.

Contents

Preface

If you were a brand-new baby sea turtle, your odds for survival would be grim: of thousands hatched, only a dozen or so make it to adulthood. From jellyfish to dandelions, this is the way nature works. Thousands of seeds are dispersed in the seas or winds, but only a few are viable survivors.

What seems to work OK in the world of nature is not effective in the world of business. Investments in workplace learning are meant to give birth to new capabilities that employees can use to improve job performance. Odds are better here than for sea turtles, but not by a huge amount. If you wanted a sure bet, your best guess would be 15% to 20% of trainees who participate in the typical workplace learning event ever employ their new capabilities in a way that leads to worthwhile results for the organization.

This book is about how people who beat those odds do so, and it is for people who want to do the same. In the past several years, we have had the privilege to work with training leaders who, despite myriad obstacles, consistently accomplish truly remarkable results. They have not done this by relying on luck or chance. They have changed the way they think about and approach their work, and they have changed the way training works in their organizations. In this way, they have helped their organizations be more successful and accomplish valuable business goals with far more certainty and speed. They have also changed the way they are perceived and valued, moving from being simply training administrators or deliverers to being impactful leaders who have earned respect and recognition.

Their results are dramatic, doubling and often tripling (and more) the return on investment from training initiatives. For the past four years, we worked side by side with these training leaders, talked with them, analyzed their approaches, and otherwise sought to understand what differentiates them from typical trainers. "Courageous Training" is a term we have coined and a model we have articulated to describe how these training leaders have accomplished their results. Why we chose the adjective "courageous" is explained below.

There are two principal components of the Courageous Training model: the Four Courageous Training Pillars (Four Pillars) and the Courageous Training Code. The Four Pillars is a systematic set of concepts, methods, and tools for thinking about, planning, implementing, and evaluating training that, when applied consistently, leads to workplace learning that has an extraordinary impact on business. The methods and tools of the Four Pillars are not based on guesswork or theory alone. They are practical and they have worked in myriad organizational settings, including health care, manufacturing, high technology, finance, sales, and professional services; they have worked in large and small organizations, public and private. They are derived from decades of research and best practices and from the authors' work with hundreds of companies around the globe developing their High Impact Learning (HIL) approaches. The authors have refined these earlier approaches into a more replicable and scalable process that more than forty leading-edge companies have adopted. In the past four years, these companies organized into a formal user group that collaborates to further refine workplace learning. The case examples in this book were drawn from recent work by some members of this user group.

This book not only examines the tools and methods that these exceptional leaders use, it also explores the second principal component of the Courageous Training model: the Courageous

Training Code. Many books provide advice on how to be a better business partner, how to turn training into performance, and how to measure training results and return on investment (ROI). But our guess is that among the thousands of training leaders who have read those books and attended the related workshops, only a handful (back to sea turtles again) have really been able to make those approaches work and to get the great results promised—either due to the shortcomings of the methods or due to a lack of concentrated effort to fully commit to a new approach in the face of resistance and challenges.

So what's new here? We have refined the Four Pillars and combined them with the Courageous Training Code. We had this revelation when we heard trailblazing trainers tell their stories. Like tightrope walkers, these trainers mustered their resolve and stepped out into a risky space. But it was more than simply taking a daring risk. As we talked with them, worked alongside them, and dug into their experiences, we discovered the principles and code of conduct that these leaders relied on to guide their interactions with senior executives, managers, and other stakeholders. These principles, which we condensed in the Courageous Training Code, enabled them to stay the course and steadfastly employ the Four Pillars. They had the audacity to set and promise lofty goals for their customers. Instead of about 20% of trainees applying new learning in ways that could impact business, they aimed to turn the ratio around, shooting for 80% or more.

The four members of the user group chose to write case examples from four different industries: manufacturing, health care, technology, and public education. Like the tightrope walker on our cover, these training leaders had the courage to step out into a new challenge without a safety net. Like a successful high-wire performer, they relied on proven techniques and practices, and they took their first steps on a small scale that they could master. They did not start out trying to cross the Grand Canyon. But they also faced risk and all acknowledge the fears they had to overcome to try the metaphorical tightrope walk in the first place.

Besides their willingness to follow a bold course, there is nothing unique about the courageous trainers that differentiates them from anyone reading this book for guidance. They are training directors, managers in training departments, chief learning officers, or human resources development consultants tasked with a principal responsibility for helping organizations plan and conduct employee learning and development. The advice and counsel, tools and methods of Courageous Training can be used by anyone who sees a need and has the resolve to make a difference. Those who take this journey will be able to improve training outcomes and raise their personal stock in their organizations.

1

Introduction: The Hole We're In and How We Can Stop Digging

The first rule for being in a hole that you can't climb out of: Stop digging!

DENIS HEALEY, former British Chancellor of the Exchequer

What if training really had to work? What if your organization was "betting the business" on a new strategic venture, the success of which depended largely on training? Could you guarantee that the training would absolutely, positively work to drive performance and to create business impact?

The odds would be against you. The reality is that training fails to work far more often than it works. If you put a hundred

1

employees through the typical corporate training program, chances are that less than 20% will end up using what they learned in ways that will lead to improved job performance. The vast majority of trainees will fail to improve their performance, even if they tried to utilize the training. They will encounter a combination of obstacles, including indifferent bosses, crushing time pressures, lack of incentives to change, peer pressure, or some other problem that will extinguish their motivation.

Why is this so?

We know what some of the causes of poor training outcomes are *not*. We know that training leaders, managers, and employees are *not* trying to make training fail. (Throughout this book the term "training leader" denotes the role that provides leadership to the learning and development function in an organization, such as training manager, chief learning officer, consultants, and other human resources development professionals whose job it is to provide direction to the workplace learning operation. The term "training" includes all workplace learning, whether in the classroom or on-line, such as employee development, leadership and executive education, technical skills training, soft skills training, job rotations, and so forth.) Training leaders do not get up each morning with a pledge to try to make things worse and to see what new disasters they can bring about. Most training leaders, moreover, are not content to see training yield suboptimal results. In fact, they work hard at trying to make sure that the training is the best it can possibly be and that trainees get as much as possible from the workshops and other learning services.

Further, we know that training leaders are not ignorant. Increasingly, they have advanced degrees in human resources development or a related field. Most of them are well educated, attend professional conferences, and read multiple books and articles each year about improving learning and performance. But several insidious forces prevent training operations from producing more than only the most marginal of business results. These are very strong, deeply rooted forces that block improvement and derail efforts to make things better, seeming to paint training leaders into a corner where failure is inevitable. This chapter is about those forces and sets the stage for the Courageous Training approach: a proven model and set of principles for action that bold leaders have used to overcome the negative forces and thereby to achieve remarkable impact and value from training investments.

One of the first things these courageous leaders did was to recognize the negative forces for what they were. The leaders also decided that they were not satisfied with business as usual. Good enough, for them, was not good enough. They began to work with their clients in ways that would effect change, using innovative methods and tools that would help ensure increased impact and value. But we also know from our work with these highly effective training leaders that the tools and methods alone were not sufficient to achieve outstanding results. The leaders also had the courage—the leadership backbone—to stand up time and again to the forces that would try to paint them back into a corner from which their efforts would fail.

Courageous Training has two complementary and interdependent parts:

- The Four Pillars, which comprise the concepts, methods, and tools that successful training leaders have employed, and

- The Courageous Training Code, which incorporates the seven principles for conduct that guide the leaders in their personal behavior and interactions with other people.

Chapter Two describes the Four Pillars; the subsequent four chapters explain each pillar in depth, including examples and illustrations of the methods and tools characteristic of each pillar. But as emphasized throughout this book, without a courageous and bold training leader, the tools and methods of the Four Pillars, as helpful as they are, are not enough. Chapter Seven examines the other half of the formula for success: the Courageous Training Code. This code articulates the rules of conduct that put into operation the intangible but vital qualities of will, tenacity, and vision that Courageous Training leaders must embody to implement the Four Pillars. Chapter Eight introduces four bold training leaders who have achieved remarkable results—the results that first inspired us to write this book. Each of these leaders wrote a case study, and the case studies comprise the subsequent four chapters. In the final chapter (Chapter Thirteen), we outline a path that other training leaders may take to begin their own courageous journey: where to start, what steps to take, and what to watch out for along the way.

WHY ISN'T TRAINING WORKING NOW?

The courageous training leaders with whom we have had the privilege to work knew things could be better, and they were determined to make them better. They saw that training efforts often were stuck in a hole, a hole that was getting deeper and, worse yet, a hole that they themselves were sometimes a party to digging!

It is useful for us to review some of the negative forces that we, our Courageous Training colleagues, other authors, and probably many training practitioners have seen that make the training hole ever deeper. These are the forces that we must recognize and understand if we are to put down our shovels and climb out of the hole into a space of Courageous Training.

The Mr. Goodwrench Syndrome

Mr. Goodwrench is the name used by an American automobile company to market its garage and repair services. It is a label that also reflects an attitude common among managers in many organizations—the notion that the training department is some sort of "employee repair" facility. According to this ingrained, habitual belief, if your employees are not performing well, then you can send them to get some training, where they will be "fixed." When the training is over, they will return as fully functioning and effective performers.

Of course it does not work this way. Almost always, the causes of poor performance that drive a frustrated manager to request training for an employee are complex and rooted in myriad organizational, cultural, and systemic issues. Lack of training is seldom the exclusive or primary problem, and a training class alone will not make the poor performance go away. The training function, despite well-intended efforts to get at real causes, is often pressured to deliver some sort of training. Very often, training leaders cave in and, against their better instincts, go ahead and fill the order for training.

And so some training is delivered, and the net results are predictable: frustration all the way around. The employees who are having difficulties do not get the real causes of their problems addressed. They sit through training that they feel they do not need, and as a result leave even more frustrated in their jobs. The manager blames the training department for being nonresponsive and unrealistic, for wanting to take too much precious manager time for an elaborate needs-analysis process, or for delivering training that is not effective—since the employees still are not performing well. Members of the training department, in turn, are frustrated that managers treat them as simply a training order-and-delivery fulfillment function, and that managers appear to be ignorant of what it takes to really improve performance. It does not take the proverbial rocket scientist to see when this syndrome is happening. But can a training leader reasonably be expected to possess the strength of will and negotiation skills needed to address the issue in the face of certain resistance?

The Training-Impact Death Spiral

Training will lead to business impact only if freshly trained employees actually try out new skills and knowledge in their everyday job performance. Almost always, they will encounter some challenges in doing this. It is common knowledge that supervisors have a lot of influence over whether employees have an opportunity to apply training in new job tasks. If supervisors act thoughtfully and effectively to help employees try out and nurture new skills, then training will stick and lead to improved performance and results. If supervisors do not—if they neglect this support role or actively challenge it with negative reinforcement—then employees will quickly return to the old way of doing things; training, therefore, will have no impact.

But most managers are not held accountable for supporting their employees' training. They are held accountable for producing sales results, meeting production goals, fulfilling customer requests, and so forth. At the end of the year, no manager was ever told, "Your unit didn't meet its production goals and your quality was terrible, but we are going to give you a hefty bonus because you were the poster child for training support." Managers will do what they need to do in order to accomplish the goals on which they are being measured. They will not do what is perceived as a "nice to do" or a distraction from producing results—such as taking time to help freshly trained employees in their efforts to try out new skills.

Moreover, most managers have witnessed a lot of training, both for themselves and for their employees, that was a waste of time and neither relevant nor helpful. Generalizing from these experiences, they find it hard to see any future training in a new light. If they had to wager on whether some new training was going to be worthwhile, or not, chances are they would bet on "not worthwhile."

Managers with this viewpoint are unlikely to take any concrete and focused actions to support the training, beyond letting employees participate. As a result, their prediction becomes a self-fulfilling prophesy: that is, the training will not be applied, and their lack of action to support it will be justified. Of course, they will not recognize that their own lack of support prevented the training from working. They will simply consider themselves prescient: "See? I didn't think this training would be worth supporting, and I was right. I don't see any results from it."

And so the downward spiral picks up speed. As managers withhold support for training that they suspect is not worthwhile, their predictions come true. As they see more evidence that training is not working, they are more reluctant than ever to change course and provide active support. Because the majority of training yields less and less impact, training leaders find it harder and harder to get managers to change their cynical attitude toward training. Eventually, it often happens that both parties simply give up. The Death Spiral claims another dance partner.

The Myth of Training as a Silver Bullet

The training-as-the-silver-bullet myth is the logical extension of the Mr. Goodwrench Syndrome and the Death Spiral described above. This myth stems from the wishful thinking that if organizations provide outstanding programs that are engaging and well-designed, then participants are very likely to take what they learned and apply it back on the job in ways that will improve their performance and organizational results.

Much has been written in the past ten years pointing out the shortcomings of this myth, encouraging training departments to position learning as a process and not as an event, and advocating substantial involvement of senior leaders and line managers if the organization is serious about sustaining a change in behavior. Despite these admonitions, however, we find that many training departments still invest a disproportionate amount of time, energy, and resources to ensure that training is a "glow in the dark" event. They fail to make even modest efforts to rigorously manage the environmental factors that are required to foster and support the use of the new skills back on the job.

Admittedly, altering the relevant environmental factors in an organization is difficult to achieve: it requires additional resources and, importantly, significant demands on managerial time and attention. Many training leaders are likely to give up putting the components in place that go beyond the training event at the first sign of the inevitable resistance from harried managers or training participants.

But the problem runs deeper than reluctance to overcome resistance. We believe that many training professionals fail to recognize and implement the key element in the concept of making learning truly a performance improvement *process*. Efforts are often made to add before- and after-training components, such as brown-bag lunches and refresher CDs, desktop job aids or laminated reminder cards, and so forth. These efforts are noble and are moving in the right direction, but they are not sufficient and contribute only the most marginal results. The real key to turning training into business impact is not in giving trainees another dose of the learning content or reminders to use it, but in ensuring that the barriers to applying learning on the job are removed or reduced. Meeting this challenge requires substantive work with and contributions from the managers of trainees and very often from the senior managers. We find that few training professionals have the access, commitment, and tenacity to stick with this work. Isn't it easier and more within our control simply to polish up the training and make it even shinier, than to confront line managers about their role in supporting performance improvement?

Butcher, Baker, or Candlestick Maker: What Business Are We In?

Many forces converge to put greater pressures on training departments: increasingly complex work processes and technologies that require constant skill updates, more diverse workforces with varied educational and cultural needs, the need to lure top talent from a decreasing pool of prospects with promises of career development and other learning benefits, and expanding regulatory and ethical rules. This is only a partial list, but it demonstrates the broad scope of demands that training departments face.

In this pressure-filled context, the tactical challenge of merely filling service orders becomes an overwhelming issue for training departments. Even though training needs are diverse and some are far more strategically vital than others, all training gets lumped together as just "training." Some training is clearly vital for execution of strategy, improving operations, launching new products, or penetrating new markets. Other training (e.g., open enrollment courses and electives) may be less vital. Regardless of the strategic level of the training inquiry, it is difficult for members of the training department to turn away requests. In some organizations, they may fear political fallout for doing so; in others they may be reluctant to lose control over training programs. They may fear that if some programs are taken away, then later they could lose them all. So despite learning department mission statements to the contrary, training is increasingly construed as a "delivery" function versus a strategic, business-enhancing process. The consequences of this misperception are troublesome.

The beleaguered training leader cannot be blamed for spending inordinately more and more time merely on managing delivery requests and issues. Take time to be a business partner? I'd love to, they might say, but I have too many other priorities right now managing and delivering training. The effort and courage it will take to go against the grain and say "no" to better focus on producing business outcomes seems too daunting.

Too Much Effort on Trying to Please "Customers"

Rest assured, we are not proposing that training should aim to annoy and displease customers. But we do see a lot of confusion about who is the customer of training, and subsequently about just whom to please. Many of the practices in a training department would lead you to believe that trainees are the principal customer group. Trainees are asked at the end of every learning engagement—a workshop, a web module, a seminar—to rate the extent to which they were pleased with the learning event, the extent to which it met their expectations, and so forth.

There is nothing wrong, of course, with efforts to make the learning experience enjoyable and to situate it in a pleasant venue. But there is something deeply wrong with being fuzzy about who the customer of the training operation really is. If the purpose of training is construed principally as a staff benefit— to provide learning and development mostly to attract and retain employees—then conceiving the training operation as if it were a university campus or commercial conference center is just fine. But the original and overarching purpose for workplace learning is to help the business perform and succeed. Given this strategic purpose, the ultimate customer is executive leadership; the proximate customer is line management—the bosses of trainees. It is their needs first and foremost that should be served. But far less attention is usually devoted to these folks.

A further but more subtle dysfunction stems from basing the training operation on a customer-service foundation. Training is only partially a service operation. In its most strategic manifestation, it is a partnering and consultative function.

The most important operational priorities of a training function should be to analyze business needs and issues, to plan and implement learning interventions that will address needs and issues, and *then to do everything possible to ensure that learning-acquired capabilities get applied in improved on-the-job performance.* Because of the separation and the compartmentalization of the training department, one of the most problematic tasks is helping to ensure the transfer of new learning into performance that drives business results. And the key to attacking this big deficiency is to engage the line manager customer (bosses of trainees) as partners and co-operators. In contrast, a customer-service focus implies that the customer need only sit back and be served. In the training business, if we are to expect and achieve results, nothing could be further from the truth. The trainee-manager customer needs to get up, pay attention, get on board with the goals of the training, and play a very active role in making sure that the goals are achieved. Any conceptual models and frameworks that point the training department away from this reality are headed in the wrong direction and dig the low-impact hole deeper.

Irrelevant and Suboptimal Metrics

One can review decades-old issues of training publications and programs from professional association conferences and see that the topics of measurement, assessing impact, and program evaluation were hot topics. Today, they are still hot topics. Training leaders have yet to figure out and adopt practical methods for measuring impact. Rigorous methodologies are available, but they are mostly too complex and expensive. On the other hand there are simpler methods, such as quarterly follow-ups and automated surveys of trainees and their managers, that tend to be quicker and easier for the training function. Because they put a burden on trainees and their managers, however, they frequently are plagued by low response rates and often produce only superficial, subjective, and unverified data. This shortage of useful, practical, and valid measures has led to widespread over-reliance on simple measures, which perniciously drive training operations in the wrong strategic direction. The most common measure is the end-of-session trainee opinion survey (sarcastically referred to as the "smile sheet"), which is used by most training functions for nearly all of their training programs and services. This simplest form of training measurement, has very little to do with genuine business value or impact and tends to distract training departments from devoting evaluation efforts on what really matters: did the training help trainees improve capability and performance and produce a positive outcome for the organization? In the absence of other measures, however, trainee opinion scores have become a substitute for evaluating effectiveness.

Once these scores take on any form of importance in an organization, behaviors to boost the scores are bound to follow. Unfortunately, almost none of the actions and improvements that can increase trainee satisfaction scores actually drive improvements in value or impact. Efforts and resources are devoted to making the training event itself better, but considerably more organizational value could be generated by investing these resources in helping trainees apply their newly learned skills more effectively on the job.

A second category of measures for training efficacy are related to costs. These measures also divert attention away from useful evaluations of training. Reducing costs is almost always a good idea but only as long as you still get what you needed when you made the decision to pay for it. Most training-cost decisions, however, are made in the vacuum of few or no impact measures. This is dangerous. If you have no idea what you are getting in terms of value, then the lower-cost service always looks like the better deal.

A third set of measures that training departments gravitate toward out of convenience (and maybe desperation for some hard metrics) revolve around enrollments. Because training budgets are based on the number of employees to be served, filling seats in training classes and earning positive reviews displaces more serious metrics, such as whether business needs are being met or performance improvements are being achieved. When it comes time to seek or justify training budgets, the common approach is to show how many employees received service: that is, how many training hours were provided, workshops delivered, or training classes completed. In fact, however, the hours of training provided and numbers of employees served are cost metrics. There is no escaping the fact that an hour of training provided is a cost, and an hour of trainee time spent in training is a cost; neither metric says a whit about value or results. Should training leaders shun these misdirecting metrics and, instead, stick their necks out to be evaluated on (and held accountable for) business impact achieved?

Sell, Sell, Sell!

Training leaders are trapped by organizational budgeting realities that operate across all economic conditions, but especially in tough economic times when training leaders attempt to fend off attacks on their budgets. They try to stretch their resources to serve the largest-possible audience and to keep their per-employee costs at what will be viewed as a reasonable level. Once in this defensive mode, they initiate efforts to enlarge their audience, to improve capacity utilization by getting more seats filled in each class, to fill orders for training quickly and efficiently, and to expand their product line to increase enrollments and please all interests. In short, they begin to travel down the sales and marketing path of drumming up more training customers and business, creating glossy course catalogs or slick web sites to drive up the number of training classes and participants. These sales and marketing efforts get in the way of the essential goal for the training department: to increase organizational effectiveness and results by improving employee capability and performance on the job.

Selling in its highest and best form is aimed at being sure customers get what they need and what will serve them best; selling in its more pernicious tactical form aims to maximize the distribution of services and products. As training leaders feel pressure to show that their services are being used and thus at least nominally to justify their budgets, the more pernicious sales efforts gain momentum. The goal of becoming a trusted advisor to the business becomes only a faint memory. Would it be principled courage or foolish bravado to attempt to defend one's budget on business results achieved rather than number of people trained?

Satisficing: Settling for Good Enough

The term "satisficing" was coined by Herbert Simon, who was awarded the Noble Prize for Economics in 1978 for his pioneering research into the decision-making process within organizations. In broad terms, the concept is used to define a decision-making approach that accepts a "good enough" option that meets the minimum requirements versus one that aims to maximize results. As discussed above, the training function is spread thin across the task of delivering a wide array of learning initiatives. When new strategies, regulations, systems, or technologies loom on the organizational horizon, there is a knee-jerk response to get the word out, to get everyone on board, to get everyone singing from the same sheet of music, and so forth. In other words, the focus is on getting the training done fast, rather than making sure it yields the maximum business impact.

Faced with the continuously increasing demands for training and all the pressures we have described in this chapter (e.g., the Mr. Goodwrench Syndrome, the Training-Impact Death Spiral, and the need to meet a variety of training requests), training leaders encounter daunting obstacles to doing things the right way. Self-survival dictates doing just enough to cover all the requests and to get things done: that is, satisficing. Combine these pressures time after time, program after program, initiative after initiative, and soon even the most optimistic and competent training leader will make compromises in order to get by. After all, if the training sessions are engaging enough and educational enough to earn good reviews and if all the budget constraints are honored, things will be OK. Executives and line managers won't give us the time, resources, or support that the training needs, so we can't worry about whether this training will actually produce measurable results for the business. Isn't the tenacity and conviction required to fight the constant battles more than can reasonably be expected from mere mortals? And so perfectly mediocre wins the day.

AT THE BOTTOM OF THE HOLE: A CULTURE OF LOW EXPECTATIONS

The forces and practices described above combine, though subtly and over time, to deepen the hole that training is in and to perpetuate the pattern of marginal returns from increasingly larger investments in training. The investments yield far less business impact than organizations need to be competitive and successful—far less, frankly, than any organization should expect and settle for.

Paying Too Much for Too Little

The limited business results produced by the small proportion of trainees who actually use their training are far too expensive. Costs of training are spread across all participants, regardless of whether they use their learning to improve job performance or not. But the return on this investment is realized only in that proportion of employees who apply learning effectively on the job. Imagine that the fully loaded cost per trainee is $2,000 for a training event and that 100 trainees participate in the training. The total cost for this training is $200,000. Imagine further that only twenty of the 100 trainees end up using their training in important on-the-job applications that yield value—a highly probable result. Looked at from a cost-per-impact perspective, this training actually costs $10,000 per trainee, far more expensive than the reported cost suggests and far too much for the gains typically realized. No wonder training departments stick with a per-trainee cost budget!

The real issue is *not* that companies are spending too much on training overall. Instead, the real issue is that they are spending far too much when the returns they are getting are just a fraction of what they could and should be.

Too Much Money Left on the Table

In one instance of poor return on investment in training, a company that manufactures construction equipment conducted marketing training for its directors and managers but only three trainees out of a total of thirty implemented their training. The good news is that they used it to such worthwhile effect that they produced results worth hundreds of thousands of dollars in increased revenues. The bad news, however, is that the training was wasted on the other twenty-seven trainees who did not make use of it. Not only did the company have to pay for their training, but it also had to suffer the expense of their lost productivity while they were in the training that they did not use. Adding insult to this injury, their managers probably were further convinced that training does not pay off, since they saw no benefit from the training they paid for.

But the biggest loss to the company that sponsored this training was the lost opportunity to gain more financial benefit from application of the training. Had the training leaders and other stakeholders worked more effectively together to identify and address problems that blocked application of the training, they might have seen another three, six, nine, or perhaps even a lot more participants use their training. Had merely six more of these non-appliers of training used it just half as well as did the top three users, the return on investment (ROI) for this initiative would have doubled.

The bottom line at the bottom of the hole is that too many of us—training leaders, managers, employees, and senior executives—expect too little from training; we are too satisfied with the relatively marginal results we are getting. We know from our evaluation studies that training has sometimes had a profound and lasting effect on people, changing their performance in ways that matter a great deal to them and their organizations. The problem is *not* that training does not work well when it works; it is that it does not work that well often enough. Training successes should be the norm, not the exception.

Courageous training leaders are ready and willing to confront this truth. They are ready to climb up on a platform and promise more. They know that the most disturbing consequence of training that does not work as well as it should is the missed opportunity to increase competitive advantage and success for their organizations and their employees. They also know that to get training out of the hole it is in, they must have the vision and courage to confront and change the practices and mind-sets that keep making the hole deeper. The Four Pillars are the platform these bold leaders stand on to ensure their learning initiatives help produce measurable business impact for their organizations.

2

What Is Courageous Training?

A STORY OF COURAGEOUS TRAINING

We start this chapter with a brief but illustrative story about Courageous Training. We then dissect the story to highlight the key elements that characterize the Courageous Training model.

PAT WILLIS'S LEARNING AND DEVELOPMENT (L&D) DEPARTMENT, like the entire company, had fallen on hard times. Increased competition and other factors had slowed sales, and all budgets were under scrutiny. A wide-scale company downsizing had resulted in leaner staff operations, and overall training enrollments had dropped consistently for the past three years. Taking time for training, it seemed, was getting harder and harder to do.

So when Pat received a call from a Senior Vice President who directed the company's global operations that important training demands were on the horizon, she hoped this was a sign that things were changing. Her budget had been under a lot of pressure; she already had to let one staff member of the training department go; and there were persistent rumors that the company was looking at outsourcing several operations completely. Training, she knew, could likely be one of them.

The meeting with the Vice President was like a breath of fresh air. This Vice President's division had just completed several acquisitions to help expand the company into Asian markets. The division also was launching a new sales strategy to work more closely with channel partners and to sell integrated, more comprehensive solutions to customers. Both of these strategic elements would require far greater than usual collaboration among members of the sales group. They would have to reach out not only across internal company boundaries, but also to channel partners and suppliers to bring more comprehensive, vertically integrated components into their sales proposals.

These new behaviors, the Vice President knew, were very different from the behaviors that had made the sales group successful in the past. New mind-sets, new skills, and new ways of working would be required. And it had to happen quickly, as the market was moving rapidly. The scenario the Vice President posed to Pat would entail several multiday training interventions for more than 2,500 employees in the current and newly acquired operations. Doing the rough math quickly in her head, Pat could envision a training rollout that would easily involve more than 5,000 training days—a huge increase in her scope of operations. In short, this would be a major "sale," significant enough to elevate her stature in the company and easily sufficient to justify reinstating her department's lost position and perhaps even adding one or two.

The Temptation of Pat

We interrupt the story for a quick review. Here's what we have so far:

- Pat's position and reputation in the company were more at risk than ever. The L&D department had descended from a major and "integral to the business" role to more of a minor and "commodity-like" role; its future looked grim.
- Her enrollments were consistently down, putting budget renewals at risk.
- She was hungry—perhaps even desperate—for a "win."
- The Vice President's request for a lot of training could save the day for her, dramatically expanding her department's scope, budget, and life span.

It would be hard for a put-upon training leader, perhaps even one for whom things were going great, to not be salivating over what might be a great coup. The Vice President is pushing hard for quick service and an aggressive rollout schedule for getting training to a lot of people as quickly as possible. For an external training sales person, the magnitude of the potential order would be measured in the millions of dollars. For an internal training leader, the sales opportunity would be equal to that amount in scope and importance, though not measured in exactly the same way.

Back to the Story: Pat's Courageous Action

FIRST, PAT TALKED WITH THE VICE PRESIDENT about the business stakes involved. Both she and the Vice President knew the stakes were obviously very high, but Pat wanted to be sure they each saw the issues in the same way. She wanted to be sure she understood how this strategy would be measured, what the major business challenges were, and how the new organization must operate. She also wanted to make sure that each recognized the potential benefit if the training was truly effective (that is, a sales force that was clear about the sales strategy and capable of selling value to the market) and the potential consequences if the training did not work (that is, failure to execute the sales strategy and likely permanent loss of the opportunity to establish a competitive beachhead in these emerging markets).

Next, she suggested a much more modest plan for the rollout of training. The Vice President initially suggested that she establish a crash task force to design a brand-new training initiative to be delivered on a rapid schedule to all 2,500 employees. Pat countered with a plan to even more quickly develop the training components and provide them to a strategically selected and vertically integrated sales group—consisting of fewer than 200 people—on a pilot basis.

She would precede the pilot training with teleconferences with each member of the senior leadership team who directed the overall Asian market initiative. In these calls, she would get the participants to identify the business success metrics by which the entire market initiative would be assessed, and to which she knew her training must directly contribute. She would be alert for consensus and agreement among the team, and plan to help the members resolve any lack of alignment or unclear expectations. She would close this phase with a commitment that her success should be gauged by the extent to which she helped drive these metrics, the same way that any other partner's work would be judged.

Following these discussions, she would capture the business goals for the initiative in an "Impact Map," which would make clear exactly how each job role that was represented in her training audience would be expected to use the training on the job in order to help drive the agreed-upon success outcomes. (See Chapter Three for a detailed discussion of Impact Maps.) She would also identify and explain the actions that the trainees' managers must take to help trainees actually use the training in the ways intended.

Pat then suggested to the Vice President that her L&D team convene web-based teleconferences with small groups of the sales managers to review the Impact Maps to be sure that they understood the business stakes involved and how the training was intended to help their sales groups succeed. As a part of this teleconference, L&D would also briefly instruct the sales managers on actions they could take to help ensure that their sales teams were successfully using the new skills and focusing on the execution of the sales strategy. Finally, L&D would provide the managers with a template and suggestions for how they could conduct brief one-on-one discussions with their direct reports who would be participating in the training. In these one-on-one discussions, the managers would be asked to explain their expectations and to help each trainee arrive at a clear plan to leverage their individual learning into job tasks that would help them and the business succeed. She included in her plan a provision for managers to access on-line coaching tools that they could use after their direct reports were trained, pointing out again the stakes involved if this training were not successfully implemented on the job.

She also recommended a brief follow-up conference call with the sales managers within one month after the training, in which they would discuss what was working well and how they were working with their teams to coach the new approach. They would also identify any obstacles they or their teams were encountering.

The final element in Pat's first rollout plan was a quick follow-up evaluation to find out how well all of these elements were working. She would survey trainees soon after training to encourage them to report what they were using, what they were struggling to use, or what they were not using at all—and what, if any, progress they were making toward executing the new sales strategy. She would focus the evaluation especially on barriers that the newly trained staff members were encountering, and she would relate these barriers to the extent to which managers and senior leaders were, or were not, providing the kinds of support that Pat knew would make or break the successful execution of the sales effort. But she would also identify other factors and management actions that were helping to reinforce or support the new skills.

Pat assured the Vice President that she could get all of this done quickly, because she knew the business plans needed rapid execution. She could move quickly to get the senior leader and manager alignment work done, and to prepare and train the pilot group. She emphasized to the Vice President that there was only one real criterion by which her work should be gauged. It was not whether she got a lot of training designed and delivered; it was not how many people she could put through training quickly; it was not whether people liked her training. The only criterion that mattered was whether her actions helped the Vice President and the Asian sales group achieve their business goals and whether the sales strategy was being executed as it needed to be. Period.

What Happened to Pat's Plan

NOT EVERY PART OF PAT'S PLAN WORKED as outlined. The senior leadership group had some disagreements about the overall business strategy that did not surface until Pat began to dig into the group's expectations. Two of the directors were not sold on the reliance on channel partners that the strategy envisioned. They wanted more company autonomy in closing financial agreements with channel partner companies. It was clear to Pat that their disagreement was likely to lead to a failure to support the strategy. She and the Vice President revised the pilot plan to exclude these directors' employees from the first round of training until they could resolve the issues.

When the managers learned of the plans to involve them in the teleconference sessions, they pushed back hard, going straight to the Senior Vice President to voice their complaints about the time commitment. Pat only learned of this when the Vice President told her that he was removing the budget for the teleconferences. After Pat agreed to revise the teleconference from ninety minutes to sixty minutes, she got the budget and the plan reinstated. (As it was, only about two-thirds of the managers actually participated. But that was enough participation for Pat to demonstrate in the evaluation that manager participation was one of the principal elements that enabled the new skills to actually be implemented post training on the job.)

The training itself had to be rescheduled because some marketing expositions that Pat had never been told about conflicted with the training dates. These schedule changes required her to combine the training into a day-and-a-half session followed later by a single one-day session. Initially, Pat had wanted three separate days, interspersed with action learning assignments involving actual account plans. As it turned out, only slightly more than half of the remaining action learning assignments were completed, as many managers never followed through on their promise to ensure that their sales teams' plans were completed. Again, though, this was enough for Pat's evaluation to identify the positive effect these assignments contributed to the success of the training and sales strategy.

Overall, the training led to mixed results. It worked very well for some sales units, and not for others. Where it was working, there was strong evidence that applying the training made a significant contribution to helping the sales regions execute the sales strategy. There were also many positive lead indicators of success, such as more solution-based proposals presented to customers, more proposals by channel partners, more penetration by the newly assembled cross-functional sales teams into new accounts, more C-level appointments made within customer organizations, a few early and large sales, and so forth.

Within a quarter of the sales districts, there was little if any execution of the strategy. In these units, there was simply too much resistance to take the time to go in a new direction. Pat was able to report that this resistance was tied directly to a failure to participate in the support activities she had included, such as the manager teleconferences.

The upshot of this story was that the Senior Vice President was encouraged by the tangible results he saw in several districts; he realized that execution of the new strategy involved challenges that he and his senior leadership team had not anticipated. He came to see that the new go-to-market strategy and the skills necessary to execute it required a bigger change than the leadership team had initially envisioned. There was still commitment to the strategy, and the evidence that it was working helped to bolster this commitment. He also learned about some high-leverage factors that either make or break the success of implementing the training in each region.

THE FOUR PILLARS OF COURAGEOUS TRAINING

From our work with dozens of Courageous Training leaders, such as Pat in our story, we have identified four principal pillars for action that characterize and support the Courageous Training approach. These are:

1. Be a business-goal bulldog.

2. Build whole-organization responsibility for training impact.

3. Win the hearts and minds of make-or-break partners.

4. Tell it like it is with truthful measurement and evaluation.

We will briefly define the Four Pillars referring to the story of Pat to explain and illustrate each pillar. Some readers may be tempted to focus on the tactical elements in the implementation, such as: Was the training three days back-to-back or two separate sessions? Did the pilot group consist of intact work units, or did it represent a cross-section of the entire population? What were the action-learning components, and how soon after the training did they start? Was the pre-work done on-line, and how long did it last? Although these elements are interesting (and sometimes relevant to training outcomes), most of the time they are inconsequential in the overall success or failure of the implementation. To some extent they are like the fanfare and theatrics of the magician who is wildly waving his hand in the air or parading the beautiful assistant around the stage. It makes for interesting conversation but distracts attention from what really matters and what is really going on to execute the plan and achieve the goals.

Pillar #1: Be a Business-Goal Bulldog

Pat perceived her role to be that of a business partner and a leader with business responsibilities. She maintained an unwavering focus on business goals and needs. She did not see herself as someone whose principal job was to deliver training, or "sell" it, or otherwise promote and sustain a commitment to do training. Instead, she saw herself as having the responsibility to help the business be successful, using training as the vehicle to drive results. Pat passed on the opportunity to make a big training "sale" that would have, at least for the short term, enhanced her status, reinstated her budget, and made her department appear to be a responsive and diligent service provider. Alternatively, she viewed everything that guided her actions through the lens of the business and a regard for what it would take for the Senior Vice President's division to succeed.

A Courageous Training leader has a firm grasp on the needs of the business and an unwavering commitment to business success. The courageous leader is first and above all a business leader who *happens* to be occupying a role in the training and development function.

Pillar #2: Build Whole-Organization Responsibility for Training Impact

Training cannot succeed unless there is consistent commitment and action from several of the nontraining parts of the organization. Managers of trainees, for example, must provide the support, encouragement, and expectation for accountability so that employees try out training-acquired capabilities. Senior leaders must buy into and express a belief in the direction that training is steering toward. They must do this not only with words but also with actions.

Pat knew that training actions begin well before such training events as workshops, seminars, and e-learning modules. She took action to ensure alignment among all stakeholders and that accountabilities for supporting the training and the performance improvement process it drives were recognized, understood, and committed to. She knew also that once people complete participation in learning interventions, they must then practice and try out new behaviors in their work. And to do this, they must perceive positive incentives, be allowed and even encouraged to take risks, and receive feedback and coaching if needed to sustain and improve their performance.

Effective training operates as a process that involves and relies on actions from different roles across an organization. Without whole-organization commitment and action, training cannot work. End of story.

Pillar #3: Win the Hearts and Minds of Make-or-Break Partners

This pillar of Courageous Training is highly interdependent with and necessitated by the previous pillar. If training is a process that requires actions by parties external to the formal training function, then training leaders must build partnerships with the people in these roles to bring them into alignment with the training and to elicit their most effective efforts.

Pat knew that she needed others to cooperate with her and to act in concert to fulfill all their mutual interests. She worked with senior leaders, for example, to help them sharpen their expectations for the execution of the new strategy and to clarify any points of disagreement or misalignment. She worked as a business partner with the Senior Vice President. She worked with line managers to understand their needs and to help them arrive at joint expectations for her and their actions. Above all, she perceived her role as a business partner, someone who worked, like her fellow line managers, on mutually held goals and issues. She did not engage them as recipients of a transactional service, attempting only to negotiate an expectation for what she would deliver. Instead, she helped gain agreement on common *business* goals—supported with a *business* rationale— then facilitated recognition of what each manager would need to do to ensure a mutually beneficial outcome.

Pillar #4: Tell It Like It Is with Truthful Measurement and Evaluation

No training will ever be 100% perfect. Inevitably, there will be omissions, shortcomings, errors, oversights, and unexpected outcomes and consequences. Parts of it, however, will go very well. Very often, for instance, people will leave training with positive learning: that is, new ways of thinking, new capabilities, or at least current but underused capabilities reinforced and validated.

There are also predictably less-successful parts of the training process. Many trainees are unlikely to successfully apply new skills on the job, due either to insufficiently learning them or, more likely, from a failure to have the requisite incentives, support, and coaching needed to employ them. Key nontraining partners are less likely than training-function players to faithfully execute their parts of the process. The training department staff, after all, has a full-time responsibility for making training work and has considerable control over the parts of the process they manage.

Pat recognized all of these issues. She avoided the temptation to evaluate and report only the parts of the process she could control, such as how much people enjoyed their training. It would have been easy to structure training evaluation to make her department look as good as possible. But effective partnerships demand the truth about who is doing what, what is working, and what is not. Above all, training leaders have a responsibility to assess what is working and what is not as far as achieving the business results at which the training was aimed. Such truthfulness, in contrast to self-serving evaluations, is much more likely to uncover negative outcomes and failed accountabilities. No one likes to hear what they think is bad news, and messengers of such news are famous for being shot. But because important problems cannot be fixed unless they are recognized, courageous leaders do not shy away from full disclosure, and they tell the truth (the whole truth and nothing but the truth) about what is working and what is not.

These then are the Four Pillars. They are the conceptual principles that guide the methods and tools that courageous leaders doggedly employ, and they form the platform on which all actions by Courageous Training leaders are executed. Each of the next four chapters is devoted to one of the Four Pillars, providing more explanations and illustrations of each.

But there is more to Courageous Training than just process. There is the personal strength of the Courageous Training leader to do as Pat did—to make the "pillars" come to life.

THE COURAGEOUS LEADER'S BACKBONE

Archimedes is noted to have said that, given a platform to stand on and a lever long enough, he could move Earth. In our view, the courageous leader's Four Pillars provide the platform and the leverage. But Archimedes would need something else in addition to the platform and the lever, as do Courageous Training leaders who want to move the world of training in their organizations. He would also need the will, strength, and intestinal fortitude to articulate and promise world-moving results, believe they are possible, then climb up and out on the platform and stay on it despite the strong winds of difficulty and setbacks.

The platform alone is necessary, but not sufficient, without these acts of belief and will. Similarly, courage alone is not sufficient. Very often, what are initially seen as brave acts are in reality acts of recklessness. Without a careful plan, a formula for actions likely to work, and the tools and skills to accomplish the plan, bravery alone can lead to disaster. In our experience, a training leader acting courageously without the terra firma of a solid and proven conceptual base will only end up being fired, never establishing the longevity and partnerships needed to grow truly worthwhile outcomes.

We choose the concept of a backbone because a spine has to be strong, yet also supple. Courageous leaders must bend without breaking, making principled compromises, much as Pat did when she yielded to demands to shorten the manager intervention. She knew that a manager intervention was vital to having a chance at success. But she also knew that there was a great deal of resistance, and that the Senior Vice President partner would have to sustain his own political capital by showing some deference to an angry mob of managers. But she did not abandon her plan for a manager intervention, because she knew this was a key part of the process that would help ensure success. She made compromises that might weaken her chances but would not destroy them. She also designed measurement processes that would surface the truth about what role the manager intervention played in the business results achieved, or not achieved.

We revisit and deepen the discussion of the leadership spine in Chapter Seven, followed by case examples. The four case examples are written by courageous leaders who demonstrate with their real-world experience the stands they took, the processes they implemented, and the principled compromises they made to achieve truly exemplary outcomes.

3

Pillar #1:
Be a Business-Goal
Bulldog

First, a few words about bulldogs. According to the American Kennel Club, the ancestors of the lovable and droopy-jowled bulldog were selectively bred for baiting bulls centuries ago on the British Isles. In this cruel and deplorable form of entertainment, the original bulldog had to be very ferocious and so courageous as to be almost insensitive to pain. Fortunately this nasty form of "sport" was outlawed in 1835 in Britain. Since that time the bulldog has been known for being "equable and kind, resolute and courageous (not vicious or aggressive) with a general appearance and attitude that suggest great stability, vigor, strength and dignity" (American Kennel Club 2007).

We chose the bulldog metaphor for Pillar #1 because we admire the bulldog's qualities of tenacity, strength, and courage. We also admire that they are not afraid to go after big things. We admire the Courageous Training leaders we have known for

33

their similar traits. Though hardly any of them have droopy jowls, all of these leaders clamp their thinking jaws onto the business needs and goals that underlie the requests they receive; they refuse to let their conceptual grip be shaken loose despite the frantic organizational flurry in which they may become engaged. They refuse to limit their vision to narrowly defined training issues and needs but, instead, always see the larger picture of the business: its goals and its needs.

In this chapter we look closely at these valuable bulldog-like capabilities. We present a conceptual framework for analyzing and articulating the linkage between training and business outcomes—a framework that we call the Logic of Training. We explain how training leaders can use this framework as a lens through which to view all training requests and how it will help them clarify the business goals and communicate the business case for training. We also provide examples of other concepts, methods, and tools that Courageous Training leaders have used to identify business goals, clarify them, and make sure the training implementation is tightly focused. Finally, we close this chapter with a list of actions that training leaders can take to apply the concepts and methods of Pillar #1.

SEEING THROUGH THE LENS THAT CREATES FOCUS—FROM THE TRAINING ROOM DOOR TO THE BOARDROOM FLOOR

The Courageous Training leaders we have known are dead clear about what they do, and especially why they do it. We have captured their clear way of thinking in a structure that we call the Logic of Training. It is meant to answer, both in general and in regard to specific training: Why is training needed? Why is it important? What are the business results it can (and will) deliver?

These Courageous Training leaders seem to have the Logic of Training wired into their thinking. Everything that they do—explaining training needs, handling training requests, formulating training strategies—is processed through the Logic of Training lens so that questions of *why* (ends) will always be clarified before talking about *how* (means).

The Fundamental Logic of Training

The fundamental Logic of Training is deceptively simple: some employees need certain capabilities to perform their jobs more effectively, so training is conducted to give them those skills. Trainees are then supposed to return to their jobs and correctly use the newly acquired skills to perform better in their work. Eventually, so goes this logic, the company will benefit from the application of these skills in, for example, higher revenues, better-quality products, increased output, more loyal customers, decreased scrap rates, and so forth.

Figure 3.1 portrays this general Logic of Training. People (1) who lack a certain useful capability participate in a learning

Figure 3.1 The Logic of Training

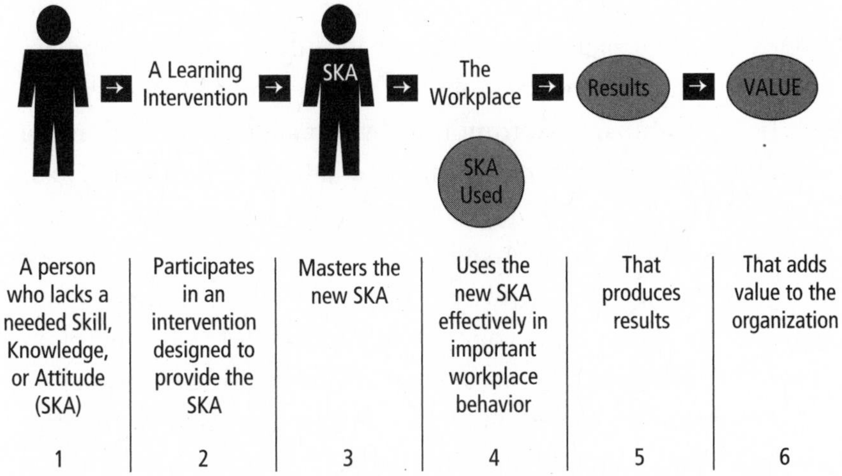
A Learning Intervention
SKA
The Workplace
Results
VALUE
SKA Used
A person who lacks a needed Skill, Knowledge, or Attitude (SKA)
1
Participates in an intervention designed to provide the SKA
2
Masters the new SKA
3
Uses the new SKA effectively in important workplace behavior
4
That produces results
5
That adds value to the organization
6

intervention (2) intended to provide them with that capability. If the learning intervention (a workshop, an on-line module, a job rotation, etc.) is efficacious, then trainees who complete it exit with that new capability (3) in their behavioral repertoire. They use that new capability in some aspect of their job performance (4). That skill application in turn enables them to produce new or enhanced results (5), which in turn contribute to some worthy organizational goal (6).

So, for example, imagine a training program that teaches service technicians to use a new time-saving troubleshooting procedure. Value to the company will occur when service technicians correctly use the new procedure, which will in turn translate into more repairs completed, more repairs completed correctly, and more problems fixed the first time. This outcome helps the company earn more profits through greater productivity; it also helps satisfy and retain customers. So, if someone asks why the company is doing this training, the answer—as viewed through the lens of the logic—is to increase profits and customer retention.

It should be noted in this example that the benefit to the organization is derived not from what was learned but from what actually gets used. This is a fundamental point in the Courageous Training paradigm: that is, value does not come merely from exposure to the training or the acquisition of new capability, but value comes from the performance changes that the training eventually leads to. This is a key aspect of the Logic of Training: the channel through which value from training is created is on-the-job performance.

It may be interesting to note that there are sometimes other reasons why training is conducted, such as to prepare employees to act effectively in an emergency, to avoid legal exposure, to bolster career development, or to meet regulatory requirements. These kinds of training have a "logic," but it is not a logic that depends on *performance change* to produce value. For example, to help recruit and retain employees in a tight labor market, a company might simply offer some kinds of training that are perceived as a staff benefit. Assuming that the employees did indeed value this offer of training, the business goal of retaining employees would be served, even though these employees might never use the training in their jobs, or elsewhere for that matter.

However, for our purpose in this chapter we will focus primarily on the logic required for performance improvement (e.g., management development, technical skills training, and customer service training), where the goal is to get people to effectively use the new capabilities on the job in ways that are important to the organization. Why do we focus on this performance Logic of Training? Simple. Because performance—effectively using learning outcomes on the job—is the principal point at which training most commonly fails. Thus, if there is anything we as training leaders need to do better, it is to get more trainees using their training more effectively in important on-the-job situations, and this is where we face the greatest need for bold and courageous actions. We focus more in depth on this reality in Chapter Four (Pillar #2: Build Whole-Organization Responsibility for Training Impact). Being sure that the business outcomes to which training must contribute are absolutely clear and accurate is the first step in driving greater application of training and results.

Training leaders typically are inundated with requests for training. Many of the presumed needs for training may turn out to need a different solution altogether, such as redesigning a work process so that it is more effective. Courageous Training leaders know that while they have to listen to and understand all of these requests, they should not always treat them as orders that automatically need to be filled. They know that requests for training are expressions of a desire for certain "ends," which are sometimes disguised as requests for certain "means."

Training Needs and Nontraining Needs

At this point, we suspect that many savvy readers are asking themselves, "When are these guys going to talk about needs analysis?" Or, "Isn't being a business-goal bulldog just another way of saying that we in this profession should be good human performance analysts?" So let's set the record straight on this right now. We are firm believers in the value and validity of human performance technology concepts and methods. They are indispensable to the training process. All training leaders should be fluent in these concepts and methods because many requests for training are not really training needs at all—as we described in the Mr. Goodwrench Syndrome. Instead the performance gaps are due to some underlying performance system issue, such as misaligned incentives, a lack of managerial direction, unclear objectives, and so forth.

In reality, the solutions are almost never all training or all nontraining. Virtually every solution aimed at improving performance will have a legitimate need for improving employees' skills and knowledge (i.e., training) tied to it, just as every training solution will need to be augmented with performance support tools, such as revised incentives, job aids, or more explicit supervisory direction. (For readers who are interested in learning more about the Human Performance Technology concepts, we suggest you visit the International Society for Performance Improvement [ISPI] web site at www.ispi.org or review Geary Rummler's work.)

Our Courageous Training approach operates from the assumption that the training needs have already been legitimately identified and verified. Our approach also assumes that even when training needs are correctly identified, training leaders still face the daunting challenge of making the training work, which entails all of the principles, concepts, methods, and tools of Courageous Training.

Digging Out the Logic

There are various reasons for conducting training, all of which may be legitimate in terms of the underlying business needs. However, the final arbiter of whether a training program is worthwhile or not is always the business ends that can be identified and served by the training. It is always wrong to move ahead with training that has an unclear, unarticulated, or indefensible business rationale. And this is where courageous leaders act like business-needs bulldogs. They relentlessly ask questions and dig into assumptions attempting to surface and clarify these business needs and issues, building the business case for the learning intervention. In other words, they clarify and test the logic of the apparent training need.

Digging out the logic means asking questions. Importantly, these questions should not be "training" questions, such as: Who do you want to train? When is the best time to train them? What competencies do you want them to master? While answers to these questions about means will eventually be necessary, they are not the questions to begin with.

Instead, the sequence of questions should focus on the business goals and issues that lie behind the request; the questions should help clarify what performance improvements are needed, from which job roles, to help improve the business outcomes. This first phase of questions should clarify the logical connections between job role performance and the business issues or goals that are the focus of the training—making sure that the connections are clear and valid. Next, the logical analysis is completed by identifying the capabilities (including skills, knowledge, and attitudes) those employees in the relevant job roles need in order to improve their performance.

Getting at Deep Business Linkage vs. a Superficial Connection

Notice that a Logic of Training analysis requires the training leader to dig deeper than simply a superficial or nominal connection, such as: "We need to do customer service training, so we can improve customer loyalty and retention." Superficial linkage that merely connects the training nominally with the nature of the business goal is not good enough. Such linkage does not specify the particular behavior and performance changes that will have to be achieved in order to truly impact the business goal. Savvy training leaders know this training pitfall and establish, therefore, a clear "Line of Sight" (i.e., a step-by-step linkage that connects the training, the job behaviors, and the specific results) through a logic analysis.

Line of Sight describes in specific terms the connection between each of the following elements:

- The key organization goals/strategy that the training is intended to support
- The team or individual results that need to be achieved to contribute to those goals
- The most critical on-the-job situations ("moments of truth") where better performance will lead to better team or individual results
- The learning outcomes from the training that will equip trainees to be effective in those on-the-job situations

Figure 3.2 shows a single Line of Sight for a Customer Service Rep. The example connects customer service training to a business goal of improving customer loyalty.

Figure 3.2 Example of Line of Sight

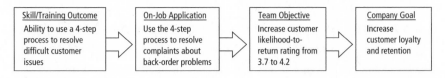

One of the most important roles played by the Courageous Training leader is to articulate the Line of Sight to all levels of employees in the organization. If *we*—as designers, facilitators, consultants, and leaders of training—cannot clearly and specifically articulate the Line of Sight, how can we expect trainees or line managers to make the connection between the training, the application back on the job, and the results? And if they cannot make the connection, how can we expect them to do the things we need them to do, like using the skills in specific, critical situations or holding their direct reports accountable for using the new behaviors?

Getting the business stakes out on the table and getting all levels of management aligned on the Line of Sight is critical for starting off in the right direction and gaining senior management's active commitment. Courageous trainers are skilled and relentless at clearly creating and communicating this business case.

GETTING THE BUSINESS STAKES OUT ON THE TABLE

An elegantly simple tool for getting the business stakes out on the table for any training or change initiative is a tool we created and named the "Impact Map." The Impact Map is a simple, graphically lean and clear tool for capturing the Line of Sight that is discovered during the logic analysis. We first employed

Impact Maps in our consulting practice as an internal analysis and communication device. We were hired by many different clients to evaluate the results achieved by dozens of different training programs. It was often the case that the clients themselves were not very clear about the specific performance and organizational goals they were hoping the training would help them achieve. For example, one large manufacturing company implemented an extensive leadership development initiative that cost several hundred thousand dollars in training materials and fees, not to mention manager time and travel costs. But beyond nebulous goals—such as improve employee productivity, increase organizational competitiveness, increase employee satisfaction, and build bench strength—they could not identify the specific outcomes they expected the training to accomplish. (Scary if you stop and think about it—but we know this training department is not alone in this predicament!) Therefore, in order to evaluate these programs, we and the client had to define and agree on the right business metrics that would accurately reflect the training's success, or lack thereof. And so we invented the Impact Map: a tabular analysis of the logic of the training on which we were focusing.

The best way to understand an Impact Map is just to look at one, as in Table 3.1. This Impact Map is one of several such maps that were created for a hotel chain that was providing training to several categories of employees. All of the training was driven by the same business purpose: to increase guest satisfaction and thus to increase return business, which is a key component of profitability and competitive advantage.

The Impact Map is laid out in columns that show, from left to right, the key capabilities the training is meant to provide to employees; the actions that employees are expected to take to apply their learning; the immediate job results that application of the learning would help produce; and the business unit and

TABLE 3.1 Impact Map for a Hotel Housekeeper Training Program

Learning Outcomes	Critical On-the-Job Actions	Key Results	Business Unit Goals: Guest Services	Company Goals
Ability to use appropriate cleaning equipment and supplies	Thoroughly clean and prepare guest rooms	All rooms fully cleaned for occupancy with no discrepancies		
	Be alert for and recognize needs for cleaning services and take appropriate action		Complete guest satisfaction	A fully satisfying guest experience for each hotel guest
Knowledge of hotel locations and services	Greet guests warmly and enthusiastically	Guest requests for service fulfilled completely and on time		
Guest relations skills	Respond completely and accurately to guest questions		All guest areas spotlessly clean and in safe and full working order	
Knowledge of emergency procedures and policies	Provide additional services on guest request and ensure guest satisfaction with response	Complete satisfaction of guest requests	Guest satisfaction scores achieve 4.2 or better on all housekeeping and staff-related items	Increase guest return rate an average of 20% across all guest categories
Knowledge of hotel standards for safe and fully equipped guest areas	Provide emergency cleaning services as needed and on request	Emergency needs met		
	Recognize and respond immediately to emergency situations			

overall goals to which the training, through application on the job, is meant to produce. Note that the entries are not lined up neatly in rows. Sometimes a single entry in one column is connected to two or more entries in another column. The connections from column to column are not preset by the training department. Instead they are discussed and determined by each user of the map based on the individual's situation and needs.

Using the Impact Map to Drive Vital Dialogues with Stakeholders

The Impact Map captures the essential logic of the training. It shows whom the training is for, how trainees are meant to use it, and why using it is important for the business. As such, it is an excellent communications tool to support a dialogue among stakeholders to help them understand, revise if necessary, and agree on the business logic for the training. Combined with the Impact Map, the dialogue can be used to explore all of the following vital questions and issues:

About the business goals

- Are these goals important?
- Are other goals more important right now; should other goals be pursued instead of these?
- What is the financial value of improvement on these goals?
- Given the likely costs for the training, how much improvement on the business goals is needed to cover expenses for the training?
- Is this much improvement likely to be achieved?

About the job results

- Are these job results important to achieving the business goals?

- Would other job results be more important to focus on?

- How are we currently performing on these results?

- How much improvement on these results would it take to make a worthwhile contribution to the business goals we are aiming for?

- Are there other more efficient and effective ways to achieve these job results (e.g., coaching; incentives; redesigning the job, tools, or technology)?

- Do the employees and their managers understand, pay attention to, and buy into these results?

About the critical on-the-job actions

- Are these the right actions to help drive the results we are aiming for?

- Do the employees know that they are supposed to do these things?

- How well are people currently performing these actions?

- Are there other more effective and efficient ways to get people to perform better on these actions (e.g., better direction, coaching, incentives; redesigning the job, tools, or technology)?

- Would learning the capabilities that the training targets help employees perform these actions?

About the learning outcomes

- Do employees already know how to do the things listed as learning outcomes?

- Are these the right things to know and do better to perform the actions needed?

- Are our employees capable of mastering these learning outcomes at the level of proficiency needed?

- Are there alternative, more effective, and more efficient ways to provide employees with these capabilities (e.g., job aids, coaching)?

Warning

Asking these questions may cause stomach upset, psychological discomfort, and possible embarrassment. Courageous Training leaders know that raising these questions and getting good answers to them is absolutely vital to the success of training . . . if success is viewed through the lens of the business, and if success is defined as making a worthy contribution to business goals. Savvy training leaders also know that raising these questions with busy business leaders and managers is time-consuming and that the people they question may have a difficult time answering. They know, moreover, that it would be a whole lot easier to skip the whole "business results" focus and just ask questions like: When would you like the training to begin?

But if training is to be effective, these questions must be raised and addressed. The questions also help redistribute more broadly the responsibility for making training work onto the other, nontraining role players, whose actions (or lack of actions) can make or break the success of the training.

Courageous Training leaders regularly raise and address these questions. When the training leaders uncover factors and circumstances that will hinder the impact of training, they address them directly with their stakeholders, helping them see and understand negative consequences that are risked. Courageous Training leaders can then suggest solutions and offer help.

Many companies provide good training, but Courageous Training leaders understand that it's not about the training. It's about the business goals and the results that training can deliver!

USING IMPACT MAPS STRATEGICALLY

The Courageous Training leaders with whom we work have pioneered a number of helpful applications of Impact Maps, and more applications continue to emerge. We list here the principal uses that have been adopted to date, and we explain briefly how each application bolsters the bold actions that are often needed to drive business impact from investments in learning and training. You will find references to many of these uses in Chapters Nine through Twelve, which provide case examples of Courageous Training.

Clarifying Initial Business Goals, Stakes, and Risks

Training leaders conduct interviews and gather information from various sources, such as web sites, quarterly analysts calls, and annual reports, to build a high-level Impact Map to show how a new or otherwise important training initiative links to business goals. Table 3.2 provides an example of such a map.

The Impact Map in Table 3.2 shows the business goal linkage for a program on leadership skills that a national beverage company requested. The map shows what participants from three different job roles—distributor general managers, operations leaders, and sales managers—would learn in the program, how they would be expected to use their learning on the job, and the resulting job and business goals at which the training would be aimed.

Winning Support from Trainees' Managers

Training leaders we work with typically construct Impact Maps that are tailored to and reflect the intended business rationale and impact for a single organizational unit or manager. They often use the Impact Map as part of an interactive session with managers that have come to be called "Impact Boosters." (We

TABLE 3.2 Example Impact Map for Overall Program

Job Roles	Key Skills and Knowledge	On-the Job Application Behaviors	Key Job/Team Results	Distributor Goals
General Manager	• Helping teams create charters and plans • Building team commitment and consensus • Using influence communications to manage change	• Build Merger Integration team consensus and commitment to corporate process standards • Empower and coach teams to review, assess, and revise distributor policies and procedures that reduce operating effectiveness	Product loss and damage at or below projected rate of 2.5%	Reduce product damage or loss (shrinkage) Achieve profit growth objectives of 18%
Operations Manager	• Coaching teams • Helping teams set performance goals • Providing team versus individual feedback	• Help sales and warehouse team leaders integrate merger-acquisition staff into teams • Help teams forecast product-handling issues and agree on proactive actions to reduce shrinkage • Assess progress and provide timely and effective coaching to teams		
Sales Manager	• Communications for coaching • Getting buy-in to aggressive performance goals • Measuring performance and providing feedback	• Help reps transition to adoption of sales tools • Help reps set and adjust shelf-space objectives • Provide coaching as needed to ensure effective application of tools	Prime shelf space in all key retail outlets increased	Achieve sales revenue increase targets of 10% Achieve market-share increase targets

explain more about Impact Boosters in Chapter Five; they are also highlighted in several instances in the case examples in Chapters Nine through Twelve.) Impact Boosters are brief sessions designed to help managers translate the overall business goals for an organizationwide training initiative into the more targeted outcomes for their own particular business unit. By cascading the business rationale and intended outcomes down to this level, which is more near and dear to a manager's heart, the training leader is much more likely to win buy-in from line management; these managers can proactively take actions to support the training and make sure that their employees not only learn it but also actually use it on the job.

Many of the Courageous Training leaders with whom we have worked have been able to take the bold action of saying to managers (in essence if not in these exact words): "OK—so now you see what the training can do for you, and we're happy to make it available to you and do whatever will help you leverage it. But frankly, whether you send your people to it or not, or help them use it or not, is your problem, not ours. You've seen the business case for it, and you know what's at stake. You're paid to make business decisions, so it's up to you."

Helping Individual Trainees Set, and Commit to, a Personalized Course of Action to Master and Apply Learning

An Impact Map can be tailored all the way down to the level of the individual trainee. It details the few most important learning outcomes that the individual plans to master in the training, then shows how that person aims to use the training on the job, and concludes with the results—both for the job and the business—to which this job performance can contribute.

Among our user colleagues, most often these individual Impact Maps are created in one-on-one dialogues between trainees and their managers (more about this in Chapter Five). Because of this, the maps become a sort of contract between trainees and their managers, subtly yet boldly off-loading the responsibility for putting the training to work from the back of the training leader and onto the shoulders of the individual trainee and his or her manager—exactly where it belongs. Many of the Courageous Training leaders with whom we work, and all of those who have contributed a chapter to this book, have taken the bold step to make individual Impact Maps a regular and distinctive part of their training implementations.

In summary, Courageous Training leaders are bulldogs when it comes to understanding and communicating the business goals of the training. They conceive of and view all of their work through a business-goal lens. They act faithfully on a pledge to do only training that will help the business, to make a clear business case for all training they do, and to not ask anything of their constituents that will not help produce business results. To them, the business rationale for training is like the marketing slogan for a well-known credit card: they "won't leave home without it."

The principal actions that operationalize the Courageous Training Pillar #1 are as follows:

1. Filter all requests for and inquiries about training through the Logic of Training framework.

2. Use Impact Maps to frame and test your own understanding of the Line of Sight that is created by connecting the intended learning outcomes, job role performance improvements, and the business results at which training is aimed.

3. Engage training stakeholders in Impact Map dialogues to create understanding and build commitment for the initiative.

4. Use Impact Maps to educate managers and explicate performance expectations for trainees that will drive outcomes that managers care about.

In the next chapter, we dig deeper into how Courageous Training leaders translate their commitment to business results into action. We also explore how they help build a shared accountability for learning and training across the entire organization.

4

Pillar #2: Build Whole-Organization Responsibility for Training Impact

A TALE OF TWO TRAINEES

LYNN AND SAL ARE BOTH NEW FINANCIAL ADVISORS working in two different regional offices. They have almost identical backgrounds: college degrees in economics, above average IQ, similar internship history, similar social upbringing, and similar financial planning education. They are smart, eager, and qualified. They also have the same problem: they are both really struggling to get appointments with prospects for their company's services. The way their business works, new advisors spend a lot of their time making cold calls to lists of qualified leads from their office's marketing manager and trying to get these prospects to come in for a get-acquainted appointment, which in turn might lead to developing their prospect into a client.

Once they have an appointment, these two advisors are good at selling; they have a similarly strong record for converting sales appointments into clients, in the top 20% for all advisors with their tenure. But they are both in the bottom 20% for getting appointments in the first place. This poor record of making appointments, despite their higher-than-average selling skills, puts both of them in the bottom 30% for sales performance—a problem for them, their careers, and their office managers.

We got to know Sal and Lynn because they were enrolled in some training that we evaluated. They attended the same three-day training workshop. The training taught advisors how to use certain proven and well-researched emotional intelligence skills to overcome internal resistance and psychological obstacles to making the cold calls that could help them obtain, schedule, and conduct more appointments. We selected Sal and Lynn (among some other trainees) for follow up and study, since each of them had also performed very well in the training on an end-of-session simulation test, and each of them also rated the training on a "smile sheet" as excellent and highly useful. But curiously, these two trainees reported very different post-training applications of what they learned. Sal used it extensively and reported a dramatic increase in cold-call success; Lynn reported almost never using the training and was still mired in a dismal cold-call performance record.

How, we wondered, could two people with almost identical capability and needs attend exactly the same training, both master the learning outcomes to the highest possible level, then report such drastically different post-training performance? We would have to interview them and dig deeper to solve this apparent mystery. We did just that and learned once again that what we think of as "training," and how we and our stakeholders define training, is often highly misguided and misleading.

Training Is More than What the Training Was

Even though Sal and Lynn attended exactly the same three-day training workshop in the same place at the same time and were even seated next to each other, the savvy training leader knows that they probably did not really have the same training experience. Our interview explored the experiences of both Sal and Lynn on several factors that began before they attended the training workshop and continued after they had completed it. What we found when we compared their experiences on this larger scale is summarized in Table 4.1. We suggest that readers first scan through Sal's experience from start to finish (in the left-hand column), then do the same with Lynn's experience. The differences that struck us as being so sharply distinct will be immediately clear.

When viewed from the larger perspective of a process that began well before each of these advisors walked into the workshop and continued long after they walked out, it is obvious that these two people did not "attend" the same training—not at all. In fact, they had dramatically different experiences, the only common part of which was the three-day training workshop. It is also clear that the training workshop, while providing some critical learning content, was greatly leveraged and enhanced (or not) by the overall process that drove the advisors participation and supported it afterward. Given their high degree of similarity in capabilities and job roles, it is also very likely that, had their experiences been reversed, then we would have documented Lynn's strong success and witnessed Sal's demise.

It's All About the Process, Not the Event

Figure 4.1 portrays the high-impact framework that we use to illustrate the reality of training impact. Although some readers

TABLE 4.1 Comparing the Actual Experience of Two Trainees Who Took the Same Training Workshop

Training Process Element	Sal's Experience	Lynn's Experience
Senior executive actions	Sal's Regional Vice President (RVP) was part of a senior executive team that helped formulate the business goals for the training. She participated in the training herself and helped deliver it in her region by making a brief presentation at the end of each workshop, telling the story of several successes she learned about through the training function's evaluation efforts in her region.	Lynn's RVP was not a fan of the emotional intelligence training or any other training for that matter. He had worked his way up in the organization through harsh experience without any help from the training department. He permitted training but did not openly profess belief in it nor did he hold his office managers accountable for developing their staff. A month prior to Lynn's training he made a video-linked presentation about the need for better sales performance and announced a new regional rewards and incentive program, but he did not mention anything about the training function or this program.
Three weeks prior to the training	Sal and his manager discussed the issues of cold calling at their bi-weekly performance phone call. Sal had looked into the training on-line, but his boss beat him to the punch, suggesting he might give it a try, since she had heard such good things about its impact from their RVP. Sal registered for the session.	Lynn and her manager met briefly to review her lagging sales performance. They pinned down the issue of cold calling, and Lynn suggested that she attend the training, as she had read about it on-line. Her boss agreed that she could attend but warned her about the risks of missing three days of cold-calling efforts. He suggested that she might think about really "buckling down hard" on her cold-call efforts instead. Lynn registered for the session anyway.
An Impact Booster session for office managers	Sal's manager participated in the Impact Booster session, and learned not only about the office business goals the training could impact, but also how to take concerted actions with trainees to help ensure their use of the training.	Lynn's manager signed up for the 60-minute Impact Booster web training that the training function led but canceled his participation when he had a conflict with time demands.

56

	Sal	Lynn
Impact Map dialogues	Sal's manager conducted an Impact Map dialogue with Sal two weeks prior to the training. They agreed on several specific actions they could both take to apply and support the training, and they defined metrics that they could use to gauge success.	Lynn tried, but failed, to make an appointment for a dialogue about the training program (an action the training department recommended to trainees whose managers missed the Impact Booster session) and sent her manager a copy of the Impact Map that the training function also provided.
Three days after the training	Sal called his manager upon returning from the workshop as they had agreed in their previous meeting. Sal reported that all had gone well, but that he might want to avail himself of the coaching his manager agreed to provide. He said he would try things out for a week, then check back in.	Lynn's manager sent her an E-mail reminding all of the advisors to think about the region's new rewards program that could earn them some enviable vacation travel benefits. There was no mention of the training that she had just attended.
Three weeks after the training	Sal experienced difficulty in sticking to the new actions and shared this reaction in a conversation with his manager. His manager, also a veteran of the same training, suggested that they download a video that the training department made available on its web site. Together they could watch this video (examples of real advisors trying the new skills) and then discuss how these examples might help Sal develop more consistency.	Lynn continued to practice some of the actions and techniques she had learned about but was seeing little progress in her cold-call record. She found the new actions awkward and difficult to stick to. She began to feel even more discouraged about how well she fit this job.
Six weeks after the training	Sal had finally upped his cold-call success by 15%, and the upward trend was continuing. He found that the strategy of setting micro-goals was working. His manager asked him to briefly describe his success at an all-office staff meeting in which they regularly reviewed training progress.	Lynn had given up and was looking for something new to help her with cold calls.
Twelve weeks after the training	Sal is regularly booking as many appointments as the top 20% of all advisors. He is now in the top 15% of advisors in sales performance. He is providing some follow-up coaching to three younger advisors who have just completed the same training.	Lynn has moved on to a new job with a different financial advising company.

Figure 4.1 High Impact Learning-to-Performance Model

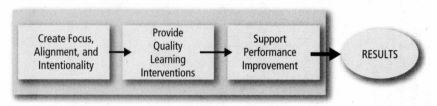

may already be familiar with this framework, it is useful to review it here. We will then turn our attention to the vital matter of how Courageous Training leaders use this model and actually make it work.

The first thing to note about Figure 4.1 is that it defines the value of training as the business results or impact that the application of the training helps achieve. Figure 4.1 then shows that this impact is determined by the efficacy of three parts of the process and how well they are integrated.

The three parts are:

- **Creating focus, alignment, and intentionality among all training stakeholders.** Many stars have to be aligned if training is going to have a chance of creating value. Senior leaders must share and commit to the business goals of the training. They must be clear about the desired behavior change and ready to hold their direct reports accountable for the actions that will be required to turn the training into on-the-job performance that is aimed at the right results. Managers of trainees also must be knowledgeable about the business goals and must commit to holding themselves and their employees accountable for using the training in important job tasks. The trainees themselves have to be fully prepared for the training. They have to know why they are going, believe in its purpose and value, be willing to try it, and have a plan to apply it that they and their boss believe in and have committed to. Finally, training leaders need to take the actions necessary to win the hearts and minds of these key players, have a plan to orchestrate all of their mutual efforts into a harmonious process, and help set and communicate realistic goals and expectations for themselves and all of the other key stakeholders.

- **Providing highly effective learning interventions and tools.** While solid learning events are not sufficient for achieving business impact, as we have noted, they are certainly necessary. The bottom line is simple: no learning, no value. If participants in learning activities do not actually master new capabilities and other learning outcomes, then it is highly unlikely that new behaviors will follow. Highly effective learning interventions and tools are almost always characterized by skill focus, active engagement of learners, opportunities and support for practice on relevant and job-specific activities, feedback, and all of the other adult learning and instructional design factors that have been proven to support effective learning.

- **Supporting ongoing performance improvement.** Learning is most fragile when it is new, since it so often competes with more ingrained behavior styles and habits. Anyone who has ever taken a golf or tennis lesson has probably experienced this firsthand. What we were able to accomplish fairly well under the watchful eye of the coach in a controlled practice session is much more difficult to execute in the less controlled environment of game conditions. Similarly, the new capability, that seemed so clear in a workshop or seminar becomes more difficult than we thought when real customers, employees, or work problems are staring us in the face. It takes continued and frequent practice of new skills to deepen and expand them, but unfortunately the workplace, with its productivity stress and demands, is a hostile environment for taking risks and trying out new things. Lasting performance improvement almost always requires coaching, frequent feedback, opportunities to try new behaviors and take risks, effective direction and goal setting, simple reminders to enhance mind-share, incentives and rewards, and so on. These follow-up methods take time and focused energy, especially when the change that training seeks is in a new direction and likely to fly in the face of the way things traditionally have been done.

Courageous Training leaders have known for years that effective training must follow the precepts of this three-part process. They know that the stories of Lynn and Sal reflect the truth about training, and many authors and researchers (besides us) have written about the concepts that underlie a process view of training. (See, for example, Brinkerhoff and Apking 2001; Robinson and Robinson 1995; Broad 2005; and Wick et al. 2006.) Our evaluation studies have uncovered hundreds of instances where this pattern was evident. And it would be hard to find a training leader who has not witnessed the dramatic fact that how much and how well employees apply their training on the job depends upon the performance environment from which they came and to which they returned after the training. Yet if this formula is so well known and so frequently written about, why does it get applied so seldom?

LEAVING IMPACT TO CHANCE, OR MAKING IT HAPPEN

Most often, training is conducted as if the event—the learning intervention at the center of Figure 4.1—were the principal causal agent for impact. This event (for example, the training workshop like the one in which Lynn and Sal participated) is carefully planned and managed. Every segment of the three-day agenda will be designed and thought through in depth. Breaks will be strategically positioned; snack and meal menus organized. PowerPoint slides and graphics will be designed in minute detail, probably receiving several higher-level reviews for format and content. Session facilitators will carefully prepare their notes and comments, sprinkling humorous anecdotes, carefully vetted for political correctness, into their presentations. Audiovisual technology will be checked and rechecked for proper functioning. Very little about training events will be left to chance. No training detail is too small to go unmanaged. But this dictum seems to apply only to the learning event itself. What about the other parts of the process?

The "before" and "after" parts of the learning process receive far less planning and design attention than does the learning event. By our calculations of hundreds of training programs in dozens of companies all around the globe, the distribution of design and planning efforts are very close to the percentage estimates pictured in Figure 4.2.

As the figure shows, the typical training program in the typical organization will receive an investment of planning and design attention that devotes about 85% to the "learning event" portion of the process, with only minor amounts of design energy being devoted to the remainder of the process. So, for example, we might find a few methods and tools tacked on to the front and back ends of the process. There might be, for instance, a communication piece provided to trainees (and maybe even their managers) in advance of the training suggesting some tips for preparing for the workshop. There might also be a brief and optional pre-work assignment. And then to help support the use of the training, the session would include an action-planning

Figure 4.2 Distribution of Investment in Planning, Design, and Effort for Typical Training Programs

Pre-Workshop 10%   Workshop 85%   Post-Workshop 5%

segment, a take-home job aid to help guide on-the-job application, and perhaps even a memo sent to managers to remind them of the importance of the training to which they sent their employees.

All of these bits and pieces are right-minded and reflect an understanding of the reality of training in relation to the issues of sustained performance and business improvement. But they are essentially just nibbling around the edges of the process and make only marginal differences.

Courageous Training leaders recognize these piecemeal efforts for the suboptimal efforts they are. These add-ons may temporarily provide training professionals with a warm feeling, since they know that they have made an effort to look beyond the training event. The add-ons, however, will not lead to sustained performance improvement and the desired results in the long run. Courageous Training leaders know that the common approach to training largely ignores the critical components of, first, creating focus/alignment up-front and, last, providing support for performance improvement—as depicted in Figure 4.1. Furthermore, it leaves any true and measurable business impact to chance.

One bold leader in our user group was quite discouraged by and unsatisfied with the business impact that a major leadership development initiative was achieving, as revealed by a Success Case Evaluation Method study he had conducted. (Success Case is a thorough yet practical approach to assess the impact of training that was developed by Rob Brinkerhoff; it is described in more detail in Chapter Six.) On digging deeper we found that the majority of the participants who were not using the training were not encountering opportunities where application of the program's concepts could be used and leveraged. In contrast, those few trainees who were using their training for impactful results were regularly and consistently involved in tasks and scenarios where the application of the program learning could make a significant difference to important business results.

The bold leader we mentioned above took the inquiry one step further by investigating the following question: "Were the opportunities and needs to apply the training just a chance happenstance, or was there some systemic cause at work?" What he found was enlightening. Most participants were enrolling for the training (or being enrolled by their bosses) when they had a relatively open period of time on their calendars. Almost all of these calendar-driven enrollees were among those who did not encounter high-leverage opportunities to apply their training. But others enrolled using far more purposive and strategic reasons for choosing when and where they participated. These few—all of whom evidenced impactful application of the training—enrolled when they were facing critical junctures in their work roles that would require application of the concepts that the program taught. One of these participants, for example, enrolled because she was about to be promoted into a new role that would require an extraordinary amount of cross-functional collaboration and cooperation—a principal focus of the leadership program. Lacking this experience, she enrolled in the session to coincide with her new move. And lo and behold, here was one of our raging successes: she applied her skills precisely when and where they were most needed, and her actions led to a dramatic new sales success that could have been achieved only with the highest degree of cross-functional interaction.

Further inquiry into this case supported the discovery that the strategic and needs-based approach was a key differentiator and determinant that predicted impact from the program. The bold leader used this data to build the business case for systematizing the enrollment process to help participants (and their bosses) uncover the business needs in their jobs that would best leverage the leadership program. This innovative change in turn drove a significant increase in the program's impact and return on investment (ROI).

The importance of having a strategic and needs-based approach was but one of our discoveries from delving into training impact and the factors that drive it. Over and over again, our training evaluation studies reinforce the lesson that training impact is only partially driven by the training event itself. The many factors and actions that create focus, intentionality, and alignment, and that help support the application of learning are extremely important in ensuring that new learning actually gets turned into important on-the-job behavior. Courageous Training leaders know this and, beyond knowing it, work doggedly to plan for and manage these parts of the training process. They know that, left to typical organizational happenstance and culture, these parts of the process will go unmanaged. They also know that, as a result, training application and impact rates will remain mired at their predictably low rates.

Courageous leaders grab the training process bull by the horns and take the steps necessary—often bold and risk-laden steps—to be sure that the entire process, not just the training event, is fully and effectively managed. They do not satisfice by just taking the training "order" and delivering a "good event," but instead they take action to ensure that the real impact-determining factors will be effectively controlled and accounted for. This means reaching out to other partners in the process, because many of these cause-determining factors lie outside the bureaucratic reach of the typical training function.

IT TAKES A VILLAGE TO RAISE PERFORMANCE

Courageous training leaders know that it is not possible for the organization to delegate responsibility for training *impact* to the training function. On one hand, they recognize that it is impossible for the training function leader—even a highly competent and motivated chief learning officer, for that matter—to control the organizational systems and segments that must be orchestrated to bring the entire learning-to-performance process into alignment. On the other hand, they do not let this reality stop them dead in their tracks or retreat into a "training as delivery" functional paradigm, leaving the impact to chance. Instead, they accept the reality that aligning the training process and making it work must be done. And they recognize that it is their responsibility to lead the effort to achieve valuable business impact. Then they act accordingly.

Tables 4.2 and 4.3 list some of the key conditions and outputs that must be present in order for training to have a high probability of consistently contributing to business results. These tables also briefly describe the actions that bold leaders take to produce the conditions and outputs needed to ensure business impact. The list of actions is segmented according to the "before" and "after" phases of the training process (see Figure 4.1) during which each condition or action is taken. Table 4.2 shows conditions and actions targeted for the first process phase of "Create Focus, Alignment, and Intentionality." Table 4.3 shows a similar list and analysis for the third phase, "Support Performance Improvement." We do not provide a parallel table for the middle phase of the process, since this is already the principal responsibility of the learning function, or, department, and thus does not entail the intensive and broad involvement of nontraining parties and roles, such as senior leaders and line managers.

TABLE 4.2 Critical Conditions and Actions Necessary for Training Impact during the "Create Focus, Alignment, and Intentionality" Phase

Condition Needed	L&D Leader Actions to Produce Conditions
• Business goals and linkage to training are clear and valid (i.e., business case for training solidly established).	• Review organization information and/or conduct interviews with key leaders and create overall linkage Impact Map.
• Senior leaders are committed to training business case and ready to hold managers accountable for application of learning.	• Review Impact Map and get agreement with senior executives or sponsors.
• Managers understand their role in ensuring impact. They are ready and willing to support on-the-job application by trainees.	• Conduct brief educational sessions with managers of trainees.
• Trainees are prepared for training, clear about targets for application and results, and accountable for on-the-job application.	• Help managers conduct brief dialogues with direct reports, using Impact Maps.
• Participation by the right trainees at the right times.	• Help managers and trainees understand and employ guidelines for effective enrollment that will ensure optimal opportunity and needs for application of learning.

TABLE 4.3 Critical Conditions and Actions Necessary for Training Impact during the "Support Performance Improvement" Phase

Condition Needed	L&D Leader Actions to Produce Conditions
• Trainees have a clear and specific action plan that is aligned with important business results.	• Help facilitate creation of plan with trainees.
• Manager and trainee have a common understanding of specific performance obstacles that are likely to be encountered in efforts to apply learning on the job.	• Help trainees identify likely obstacles and communicate same to managers.
• Managers are committed to hold trainees accountable for action plan.	• Help managers conduct a dialogue with trainees to review and agree to joint accountabilities for application of learning.
• Managers are prepared to provide assistance that helps remove, reduce, or counter negative effects of performance obstacles.	• Provide managers with guidelines and tools that will help them help trainees overcome obstacles.
• Managers provide ongoing coaching, performance feedback, and other assistance as needed for trainees to continuously leverage learning into improved performance.	• Provide managers with tools, systems, and methods that help them provide effective performance support.
• Senior leadership (and other key stakeholders) understand the business results achieved by training and factors that have supported or inhibited training impact.	• Conduct impact evaluation studies that gauge business impact and pinpoint factors that can be acted on to improve ROI.
• Senior leadership actions help all key roles take actions to improve training ROI.	• Help leaders formulate and make decisions that will improve training results and effectiveness.
• Senior leadership hold managers accountable for coaching/supporting performance improvement.	• Help facilitate a progress check with senior leaders and managers to identify lead indicators of success and obstacles.

It is clear from a review of tables 4.2 and 4.3 that it truly "takes a village" to make training pay off. When it comes down to whether and how well training will ever be used on the job in ways that will impact important results, the actions and practices of the key nontraining players (especially the trainees themselves, their immediate managers, and the organization's senior leaders) are the true make-or-break factors. The best training events in the world cannot have a whit of impact if the performance systems in the organization are aligned against them and many of the conditions listed in tables 4.2 and 4.3 are not in place.

Courageous Training leaders plan and design the training intervention from start to finish as a comprehensive and seamless process that will start with critical alignment and buy-in from senior leaders. The intervention is designed to focus on and ensure measurable performance and business outcomes and will end with truthful evaluation feedback that pinpoints what worked, what did not, and who has to do what in the future to get better (and better) business results. Leaders take it on themselves to be sure that all of the key parties in the process understand their roles and responsibilities and are aware of the stakes involved if balls are dropped. They confront the reality of the needs for these conditions to be met if training investments are to pay off. They may need to compromise on the degree and level of participation of the key parties, but they do not go forward when conditions fall below a minimum acceptable level; in these cases, they advise senior leaders of the likelihood of failure and politely recommend postponing the proposed training venture until the conditions are more favorable.

Courageous Training leaders also recognize that they have a responsibility to build the tools and methods that can help the key players fulfill their responsibilities. In short, they work hard to ensure that all of their actions—the decisions they make, the communications they disseminate, the interactions they have with key players, the plans they prepare, the programs they mount—are aligned and consistent with the overarching principle that achieving results from training is a whole-organization responsibility. We provide more depth on bold strategies and tactics for working to forge the partnerships needed to put this Courageous Training pillar into action in Chapter Five.

In summary, the principal actions that operationalize Courageous Training Pillar #2 are as follows:

1. Design a learning process that builds in roles for all stakeholders to ensure alignment and focus *before*, and performance improvement support *after*, the event.

2. Educate the nontraining partners about their critical roles in the process.

3. Deploy resources across the entire learning process.

4. Work with partners outside of training to ensure that the conditions for success are in place.

5. Use the training business case to gain commitment from managers and senior managers to perform their roles.

5

Pillar #3: Win the Hearts and Minds of the Make-or-Break Partners

A few years back we were making a presentation to a group of Human Resources and Development (HRD) professionals at a conference about various issues we have described in this book: the low proportion of training that actually gets used by participants, the root causes of failure for training initiatives, the fact that senior managers and line managers must play a critical role if training is going to produce real business impact, and so forth. We remember vividly a gentleman from a company in Boston vigorously raising his hand and posing this challenge: "I believe everything you have said in your presentation. I think everyone in this room especially knows that we need line managers to support our training. You're not telling us anything we don't already know. But we've tried over and over to get them more involved and nothing works. What can we do differently?"

His comments summed up the challenge pretty well: even if we as HRD professionals are aware of the troubling state of training's low impact, it is very difficult to get anyone outside of the training function to take the message to heart and actually do something to make a difference. But the reality remains: getting results from training is a whole-organization responsibility. Unless we get concrete and focused actions from the make-or-break players in the process, training is doomed to continue its pattern of marginal results, and the spiral of low expectations leading to mediocre results will gain speed. In this chapter we provide strategies and tools that Courageous Training leaders can employ to gain the constructive involvement of key stakeholders.

THE FOUR KEY PLAYERS

There are four key players whose actions and commitments make up the vital parts of the training impact puzzle. (See Figure 5.1.) As the gentleman from Boston so aptly put it, identifying the fact that these four players have a vital role in the drama of training impact is not necessarily news. Figuring out what we need to do to bring them together, to define and gain their commitment, to motivate their involvement, and then to sustain it— that is the challenge. To that end, we discuss and explain the role of one key player at a time, the methods and tools we have seen Courageous Training leaders use to address this challenge and to drive truly remarkable results from their training efforts.

As Figure 5.1 shows, the four key players whose involvement is necessary for increasing business impact from training are senior executives, managers of trainees, trainees themselves, and the training leader (the person or team from the training function that provides leadership for the learning initiative). The figure is

Figure 5.1 The Training Impact Player Puzzle

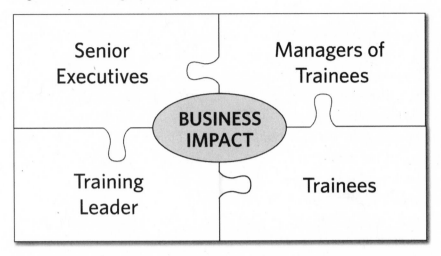

conceived as a jigsaw puzzle, connoting the fact that each of these players has a role that interacts and fits with another—and that the entire picture is not complete without each part being fully involved. At the center of these interlocking roles is the impact that the training initiative is designed to achieve. This business impact is both the purpose for the interactions of the four roles and the keystone that holds them together.

BUSINESS STAKES: THE CENTRAL INVOLVEMENT STRATAGEM

Courageous Training leaders know that they cannot beg for involvement as if it were a charitable donation to the training department or otherwise try to sell the need for participation as a sort of patriotic duty that is owed in allegiance for the good of the company. Instead they rely on a single, core stratagem: give the players a clear and valid business rationale for their involvement. They make clear what the business stakes are, how outcomes of value to each player are dependent on the actions they must take, and what will be lost to *them* if they fail to commit and act. In short, Courageous Training leaders turn the stakes around. The common approach to gaining commitment has typically been as a supplicant: "I need your help in achieving this goal for the training department." Instead, the Courageous Training leader will, as we see it, assume the role of business partner and trusted advisor: "I know this is what you are trying to achieve, and I have a few suggestions as to how you can increase the odds you will get to *your* goal." Just how the Courageous Training leader does this with each key player varies—just as the stakes and interests of each player varies. But central to each approach is getting to the core of *why* each player should care. What is in it for them if the training is successful, what they are likely to risk or lose if it is not, and what does each of them together—training leader and key role player—need to do to ensure the greatest likelihood for success. Hence, the importance of being a business-goal bulldog. Throughout this chapter we will refer back to many of the concepts and tools (e.g., Impact Maps) that help make the business case for the training initiative.

THE SENIOR EXECUTIVE ROLE

We need several actions and commitments from senior executives to make training work. One such commitment is what a client of ours calls "air cover," a military concept that provides an overall view of the battlefield and can protect combatants below from unseen or otherwise potentially catastrophic points of attack. The senior executive is the person who can best provide this air cover, helping neutralize threats that could derail the training effort. For example, in a recent training initiative in which we were working with a pharmaceutical client, line managers had previously agreed to engage in educational sessions that would give them guidance for coaching their employees after they participated in our training. But at the last minute, these managers backed out of the sessions, claiming that they had to prepare for a regulatory audit that had just been announced to them. If the managers did not attend the learning session we had designed, we knew that the chances for success of the training were seriously threatened. The skills that the trainees would be learning were new and would need a considerable amount of on-the-job coaching and support. We apprised the senior executive of the issue and reminded her of the risk to the business—a possible loss of market position and sales leverage—if trainees did not get the maximum degree of support from their managers that this session would teach and motivate them to provide. We knew also that the managers were rightly concerned about the risks posed by failing to be ready for the upcoming audit. Only the senior executive, we knew, could influence the internal regulators to postpone their audit, and this is exactly what she did. Relieved from the immediate need to prepare for the audit, managers participated as planned in our preparatory session, and the training was successful.

Beyond providing this vital "air cover," there are other conditions and support that only senior executives can provide. Establishing these conditions demands focused and carefully guided interactions by the training leader with those senior executives who are the principal sponsors and stakeholders of the training. Training leaders often construe the commitments needed from senior executives more vaguely as "support and sponsorship." While these constructs are important and every training initiative needs a senior level sponsor to take ownership, aiming only for a general willingness from a senior executive to attach his or her name to the training as sponsor is a superficial goal that glosses over what we are really trying to accomplish. Moreover, "support and sponsorship" is "training-speak," which undermines our credibility as a business partner and threatens our effectiveness. Support and active sponsorship are by-products of the executive's involvement but are not the reason why the training leader wants or needs to talk with the executive.

The overarching reason for interactions with senior executive sponsors and stakeholders is very simple. Everyone involved must be crystal clear on what the executive stakeholder's vision and business expectations are for each initiative. Training leaders and others need to be able to articulate the business goals and the metrics—how the executive, the training leaders, and the rest of the organization will know progress is being made on the goals—for this intervention. As outlined in Chapter Three, the entries in the two far-right columns of the Impact Map—Organization/Business Unit Goals and the Individual/Department Results—must be clear, valid, and deemed worthy of investment by all the stakeholders involved. Courageous Training leaders need to have a laser-like understanding of (and to be able to articulate for the rest of the organization) the goals of training initiatives and how the learning interventions will drive those results.

Understanding and articulating the business case for the training requires more effort than simply extracting it from senior leaders. Most often, the senior executives will have only a fuzzy or partial view of how the training could contribute to their vital business goals and strategies. Thus the savvy training leader facilitates a conversation with them that, first, surfaces their opinions of the most important business goals and issues facing the organization. The training leader then guides the conversation in a direction that can make connections between the performance of vital job roles and the business goals and metrics that the training—if it helps shape this performance—can link to. Finally, the training leader will confirm the vision and the business case for the training (an Impact Map is an extremely useful tool for this) so that the senior executive sponsors have a clear expectation for the business goals that the training should contribute to, feel a sense of ownership for these goals, and are committed to the success of the training in helping to achieve them.

Another important reason for the training leader to interact with the senior stakeholders is to give them some valuable information about *their* critical role in setting expectations and holding people accountable for meeting these expectations. Although the concept of setting expectations and holding people in various roles accountable is simple and logical, very few training interventions actually have these two factors operating. A focused and productive business discussion about these issues with the executive stakeholder is necessary for gaining the level of executive support and championship of the training that we desire. Such championship goes beyond superficial sponsor identification; it embraces proactive and focused actions for providing "air cover" when needed, holds managers accountable for supporting employee participation and performance, and so forth. Talking about expectations and accountability is a *business* discussion about the execution of the business strategy. Talking about executive support for the training is a *training* discussion about a training implementation. Senior executives do not have time to talk about training, but they will make time for finding ways to improve business results. Courageous Training leaders clearly understand this difference and are skilled at having the strategic *business* discussion.

Despite the criticality of business conversations with senior executives, many training managers shy away from this important stakeholder interaction because of the belief, almost reverential at times, that the executive is too important or too busy. We have heard many HRD professionals say, "We can't go to the

Vice President of Sales; he's too busy to get involved in this." He undoubtedly is busy, but the Courageous Training leader can make a compelling argument for why the executive absolutely must make time for this. Senior executives will always be too busy, as well they should be, to help a training leader solve a training problem. But, the real reason for the training in the first place is to help the senior manager execute an important strategy or accomplish a particular business goal. Getting them involved appropriately is vital to the success of *their* initiative. If we can't make a compelling business case for their involvement, then why are we doing the training in the first place?

Done effectively, a training leader's conversations with senior executives will produce a valuable by-product. The discussions will raise the bar for what the executive and the organization should expect from its training investment: improved performance leading to tangible business results. Much of the "how" behind gaining commitments from senior stakeholders is described in detail in Chapter Three. Especially relevant is the section on how to create an Impact Map and the questions that should be used in those key discussions.

MANAGERS OF TRAINEES

In our research and evaluation of countless training initiatives, we have found the direct bosses of the training participants to be absolutely critical to success. They are often the first and last voice heard by trainees in communicating the expectations and accountabilities of the training, and they are the linchpin in ensuring that the importance of the training intervention is cascaded accurately down to the training participants. Without the managers' proactive communication with their trainees, the business case and vision so carefully constructed with the senior executives will never be achieved.

From interviews with and surveys of hundreds of trainees across scores of organizations, we find that the most common reason that trainees give for attendance in a training program is that "my manager sent me." This might be a positive sign, since after all we want manager involvement. But unfortunately almost none of these trainees can articulate any reason beyond simply saying: "I am here because I was told to be here." Ask these trainees what they will learn, how they will use their learning on the job, what performance applications they will be held accountable for, or other questions about the focus and intentions of the training, and they are mostly stumped. While we might expect these sorts of inadequate responses from lower-level employees in mandatory or entry-level training, we find to our dismay that similar responses are common across supervisory training, management development, and sadly even highly expensive executive development programs.

Courageous Training leaders have recognized this ubiquitous problem, and they have decided to do something about it. They know that if the lack of trainee preparation and focus prevails, then the expectations they have helped formulate with senior executives about business impact will be seriously at risk. So, they take proactive and vigorous actions to work with managers of trainees, knowing that these managers can have a tremendous influence in helping motivate, prepare, and hold trainees accountable for using what they will learn in vital training initiatives. Over the years, we and our user group of Courageous Training leaders have learned a lot about how to capture the hearts and minds of managers on the important issue of setting expectations and holding their people accountable for using the new skills or processes. After much trial and error, we and our colleagues realized that you cannot *teach* managers about the importance of creating focus for and supporting the learning. Instead, they need to discover it for themselves, both in their heads and in their hearts. Training leaders must lead managers to this discovery in a manner that is quick, to the point, and that fits into the managers' busy schedules.

The principal stratagem used to guide the work with managers is articulating a clear and compelling business case for the training. At the line managers level, however, this means more than just communicating the business linkage for the training as it was articulated for the senior executives. The overall business case for the training will be different in each work unit of the organization and must be redefined to align with the business objectives and issues faced by each line manager. Imagine some customer service training to be provided to all employees in a large chain of hotels, and imagine further that the overall business purpose is to improve customer service so that first-time hotel guests will be more likely to become regular guests. (Repeat business is one of the major drivers for profits in the hotel business.) The manager of the housekeeping function in the hotel has different business goals and issues than those faced by the manager of conference sales or front-desk operations. If these different managers cannot see how the customer service training can be used to help them improve performance on their unique business goals, then they are less likely to buy into and support the training, beyond reluctantly allowing their employees to participate in it.

Given that each manager's business needs for the training will vary at least somewhat, it is necessary to interact with each of the managers whose employees will participate in the training. In some organizations dozens or even hundreds of managers may be involved, so our bold training leader colleagues have found that conducting group intervention sessions with managers is the only reasonable way to reach all of the managers. At hearing this news, we suspect that many readers are probably thinking along the lines of the gentleman from Boston whom we mentioned at the beginning of this chapter: "Yikes! Now you want me to run sessions for managers of trainees in addition to running the training itself? You've got to be kidding! They'll never participate in that."

Courageous Training leaders fully anticipate meeting resistance on the point of training the trainees' managers, but they are prepared to stick to their beliefs about the necessity of getting managers aligned with and committed to the learning intervention (read: *business initiative*). The same principles for building buy-in and commitment from senior executives hold true for line managers. The purpose of the solicitation of time from managers is not so they can "help the training function." It is so they can help themselves more effectively and efficiently achieve the business goals for which they are accountable. So, we make it crystal clear how the training can do just that. We have also found that once the senior leaders (i.e., the managers of these line managers) have understood and bought into the business case for the training, it is much easier to win the participation of the line mangers.

Impact Boosters

Our colleagues in the user group commonly conduct group interventions for managers of trainees. We have named these interventions "Impact Boosters" because we see them as an "additive" to the training process that boosts the likelihood of impact. We have all found that not only do these sessions indeed work to boost the impact of the training, but that managers have responded quite positively to giving their time and energy to participate in them—because they have seen the outcomes. These sessions take many forms, from one-on-one telephone conversations, to sixty-minute group teleconferences, to two-hour or longer group classroom sessions. In the case of Holcim Cement (profiled in Chapter Eleven), the Impact Booster was a full-day classroom version. For readers who wonder how on Earth a training leader sold (or even had the nerve to try to sell) the idea of a full-day session for managers to learn about what they could do to support their employees in training, we offer this fact: At Holcim, the training leader started with a much shorter version of the Impact Booster. When the managers and senior leaders saw the enhanced business value this was leading to, they themselves asked the training leader to extend the session to a full day. The business results did the "selling," and the managers convinced themselves of the session's value.

Our bold Courageous Training leaders have been very creative in forging Impact Booster sessions so that they accommodate all constraints; such flexibility ensures that, in one form or another, the sessions will happen. Some leaders, for example, have embedded the booster sessions into existing manager meetings or teleconferences. Regardless of the individual variations, however, each Impact Booster session is designed to achieve the same principal outcomes, as follows:

- Help the managers articulate and understand the linkage between the learning outcomes of training for their employees and the manager's business goals, which are in turn aligned with the overall business goals of the organization.

- Familiarize the managers with methods and tools they can use to prepare, motivate, and coach employees to apply the training in important job tasks, thus helping the managers achieve their goals.

- Help the managers identify and communicate to employees the high-leverage application of the training in on-the-job tasks for which they will hold their employee trainees accountable.

The Impact Booster sessions prepare and motivate managers to engage in two important actions. First, before the manager's employee begins the training process, the manager will meet with him or her to discuss, refine, and personalize the Impact Map, creating an individual Line of Sight that identifies key learning outcomes, actions to apply the learning on the job, and results to be expected This dialogue between the manager and employee goes a long way toward setting the expectation that the training is important and that the employee is expected to be using the new skills or knowledge.

The second action we expect the manager to take is meeting with the employee within two weeks after the training session. In this meeting the manager reviews the action plan created by the employee during the training and provides the necessary support to effectively deploy the new skills or knowledge that will lead to improved performance. The length of time required for these discussions varies, but the meeting can typically be successfully completed in fifteen to twenty minutes.

Impact Boosters Work

Our evaluation studies and the varied work of our colleagues in the user group provide ample evidence that, as we might expect, Impact Boosters are very helpful in getting managers involved in the training process. Studies also show that this pays off in improved applications of training and subsequent business results. Below is a brief summary of a research study we conducted for one of our customers; it demonstrates the power of management involvement to turn learning into important and measurable business outcomes.

A global technology company headquartered in North America had a comprehensive leadership development curriculum segmented for various levels of leadership within the organization. Some months after the training, we helped them evaluate the leadership programs to determine what was working and what kind of business impact it had helped participants produce.

Our Success Case Method study turned up solid evidence of significant and tangible business results that participants were able to produce by applying what they learned from the leadership programs. (Details about the evaluation process are examined in Chapter Six.) For instance, one manager used what she learned about cross-functional leadership to lead the development of an innovative solution that crossed technology platforms and had significant projected sales. Another director used what he learned to implement a Total Quality Management (TQM) process for fixing software bugs in his unit. He was able to document a 30% improvement in fixes that, even by conservative estimates, yielded a direct savings greater than $700,000 in less than one year, not to mention prevented customer problems and dissatisfaction that result when bugs persist.

Although the training paid off handsomely for the organization, the remarkable finding from this study was the clear connection between results and the extent to which the managers supported the trainees in applying their new skills. The study showed that 69% of the participants who met with their managing director before and after the training produced measurable and significant results; whereas only 30% of the people who *didn't* meet with their manager both before and after the training produced measurable and significant results. Studies of training in other companies represented in our user group have yielded consistently similar findings: management involvement helped double or triple the business impact of training initiatives.

Once such stories are gathered and reported in an organization, levels of resistance decrease regarding processes such as Impact Boosters and trainee Impact Map dialogues—practices that were previously thought to be next to impossible to make work. The training leader at Holcim Cement (author of the case example presented in Chapter Eleven) even experienced the seemingly incredible circumstance of managers asking her to increase the length of time that she had scheduled for their Impact Booster sessions.

TRAINEES

It is, of course, blindingly obvious that the trainees themselves play an important role in turning the learning into business results. It is the trainee who is the target of the training and is expected to acquire the new skill or knowledge and then to use it on the job. Our belief is that the large majority of employees in almost any organization are interested in trying to improve their performance and are willing to learn skills that will make their jobs easier and help themselves be more productive. So, when we find large proportions of employees not using training in ways that help them and their organizations succeed, it underscores for us the reality that we discussed in Chapter Four: most training fails to get used back on the job because there are obstacles or disincentives for using the new skills in the ways they were intended. Given this fact, when we look at how we can work with trainees to help improve the business impact of training, our focus is not on helping them learn more or learn better, but to help them *use more* of what they have learned in effective ways that will drive value.

The trainees' motivations and expectations are important factors in whether the trainees will apply their learning back on the job (e.g., Tannenbaum and Yukl 1992). Another category of factors that interact with trainees' motivations and prevent them from applying the training is the obstacles that they will encounter in the workplace, such as time pressures, lack of managerial direction, lack of accountability and measurement, and so forth. The bold training leaders we know do not merely accept the current level of trainee motivation or resign themselves to the bumper sticker notion that "obstacles happen" in the work environment. Instead, they take focused and direct action to shape and mold the circumstances to the greatest advantage. They use several strategies to accomplish this:

- Help trainees have access to and participate in a dialogue with their managers to clarify a Line of Sight that connects their individual learning objectives with valuable work unit results. This dialogue helps them recognize and adopt a valid and constructive reason not only for participating in the training but also for using it to improve their performance in ways that will yield tangible benefits.

- Engage trainees in reflection during their learning interventions. We know that trainees' initial understanding of, and intentions for using, training will probably change, so the reflection points in the workshop help them to refocus.

- Help trainees identify and forecast the obstacles they are likely to face when they try to apply their new learning.

- Facilitate the creation of an individual action plan that specifies concrete, time-specific efforts to apply new learning in the most immediate opportunities. Because the action plan is concrete, limited to just a few realistic application efforts, and linked to valued outcomes, it helps the trainee make a firm commitment to sustain the learning effort and apply the training soon after its conclusion.

- Encourage trainees to engage in a dialogue with their managers to discuss the action plan and make it a further "contract" between the manager and trainee. Here, we remind the trainees that their managers are expecting an action plan and expecting to meet and talk about it. By working both sides of the equation—manager expectations and trainee expectations—the training leader is grooming the application environment for the optimal likelihood that the training will stick and turn into improved job performance.

Underlying all of these actions, methods, and tools is the same principal stratagem: making a business case for the training, so that using it will be seen throughout an organization as a way to bring valuable results and benefits. In the case of individual trainees, the business case must be tailored to their more immediate interests, concerns, and values. But the bottom line is the same: here is why the training is important, here is what it can do for you and your organization, and here is what you need to do to make it work. Furthermore, the expectation is set that many people—their managers, the training department, their senior leaders—are not only counting on the trainees' success but also are ready to help them make it work. And the accountabilities are in place to make this work.

TRAINING LEADER

The maestro who guides this entire process is the training leader. As in a symphony, no single performer can carry the entire piece alone to produce the desired results, although at different times particular sections or individual performers move to the forefront, such as when senior leaders might intervene in providing "air cover." There is a plan and a particular sheet of music that everyone must follow. Every section must do its part for the symphony's performance goals to be met. The training leader is the logical person to fill the role of the maestro, having composed the impact symphony and being aware of all the parts and how they must be sequenced and integrated.

Continuing with the orchestra analogy, the typical view of the training process has the training leader and trainees recording alone in a studio, hoping that eventually someone will mix that singular performance (a training event) into a harmonious symphony that achieves business results for the organization.

The Courageous Training leader role we espouse changes this paradigm. The training leader is still responsible for designing and implementing a high-quality learning intervention, but the role goes significantly further to include orchestrating and guiding the critical parts to be played by the other vital partners: senior leaders, managers of trainees, and the trainees themselves. It takes courage to make the commitment to lead this new symphony process and to promise the organization's audience the elevated results, because being the maestro is a new role for most training professionals. The other players also will be asked to go beyond what their role in training has previously been, and this magnifies the risks and challenges that the first-time courageous leader will face. The good news is that the tasks for this new leadership role get less daunting as progress is achieved. Not only does the leader gain confidence with practice and success but as the other partners witness the improved performance and results that benefit them, they are also much more motivated to play their parts with increasing skill and gusto.

TABLE 5.1 Critical Actions of Training Leaders to Orchestrate Training Impact

Critical Actions of Training Leaders
Leader Actions
■ Create Impact Map with senior stakeholder input to depict overall linkage of training initiatives to business goals.
■ Review Impact Map and get agreement with senior executives or sponsors.
■ Design Impact Booster intervention alternatives that are aligned with organizational constraints and opportunities.
■ Conduct Impact Booster sessions with managers of trainees to surface and connect business unit goals/stakes to the training and to provide managers with capability needed to support optimal trainee learning applications.
■ Provide tools and other aids to help managers conduct Impact Map dialogues with direct reports.
■ Train and otherwise equip learning intervention facilitators to optimize Impact Maps and High Impact Learning (HIL) methods during learning sessions.
■ Help trainees identify likely obstacles and communicate them to managers.
■ Provide managers with tools, systems, and methods that help them provide effective ongoing performance support and address obstacles.
■ Manage, monitor, and track progress of overall implementation process.
■ Conduct impact evaluation studies that gauge business impact and pinpoint factors that can be acted on to improve return on investment (ROI).
■ Help leaders formulate and make decisions that will improve training results and effectiveness based on evaluation results.

Table 5.1 summarizes the orchestration actions that the training leader must take. These will be familiar to readers to some extent, as bits and pieces of these actions have been described in earlier chapters. The evaluation and measurement actions listed in the table will be presented in the next chapter.

In summary, we have reformulated the role of the training leader to move significantly beyond the more traditional role of managing the design and delivery of training programs. The new Courageous Training leader role takes on the expanded responsibility of orchestrating and leading a process that involves and relies on contributions from other, nontraining stakeholders. All Courageous Training leaders we have worked with have suffered some angst over assuming this new role, and none have transitioned into it without encountering obstacles and issues that have stretched their capabilities. This new role has frequently pushed them beyond their comfort zone, and yet the organizational and personal payoffs have been significant and gratifying. First and foremost, these leaders have seen, maybe for the first time, the organization accomplish many of its desired business outcomes as a result of learning interventions. They have compelling, concrete evidence that would stand up in a court of law that the specific outcomes that senior management really cares about are being achieved.

Second, the Courageous Training leaders have received feedback from their business partners in line management that the approach makes sense and is working to produce greater results. Further, they gain greater levels of commitment and support for training from these managers. Many of our Courageous Training leaders have also reported that they have seen a change in the dynamic of the relationships between the learning and development (L&D) organization and senior and line management. They are viewed as more of a partner in the business and not just a supplier of training.

Training leaders face a strategic challenge in getting their organizations to adopt the new "whole organization" approach as the way it will routinely conduct training. The key to accelerating the transformation, we have discovered, is measurement and evaluation. Nothing greases the wheels of change like evidence of how well new approaches are really working, or not working. This is the topic of Chapter Six.

In summary, the principal actions that operationalize Courageous Training Pillar #3 are as follows:

1. Use the training business case to gain commitment from managers and senior managers to perform their roles.

2. Establish accountabilities for managers and trainees with the help of senior stakeholders.

3. Educate the nontraining partners on their critical roles in the process using Impact Boosters.

4. Managers and trainees have an Impact Map dialogue to create an individual Line of Sight.

5. Trainees create realistic action plans during the training.

6. Managers meet with trainees shortly after the training to refine the action plan.

6

Pillar #4: Tell It Like It Is with Truthful Measurement and Evaluation

There's an old but still poignant story that goes like this: A young newly wed couple was preparing a large ham to roast for Sunday dinner. As the wife was putting the seasoned ham into the pan for baking, the husband asked: "Aren't you going to cut the end off it?" The wife asked him what he meant and why she should do that. The husband replied that cutting off the end from the ham was the way he had always seen his mother cook hams. Her cooking confidence now shaken, the wife called the husband's mother to query her about this ham-lopping practice. The mother replied that she had learned this from her mother but couldn't recall ever knowing the reason. The new bride then called her mother-in-law's mother, who verified the legitimacy of the practice and said she learned this from her mother; although she continued to cut the end off

93

to this day, she also couldn't say with certainty the reason for this practice. Fortunately, though very old, the grandmother (the bride's husband's great-grandmother) was still alive, well, and surprisingly lucid. A call to her cleared up the origin of the ham-trimming ritual. In an age-quaked voice, the grandmother explained that she had regularly roasted a ham for her family's Sunday dinner. She went on to explain that they had a very large family and so she had to purchase a large ham to feed everyone. Because the ham was always so large, it wouldn't fit in her only roasting pan. And a larger roasting pan wouldn't have fit in her small oven. Therefore, she did indeed trim the end off—so it would fit.

Over our many decades of work with training departments and leaders around the world, it has struck us that a good deal of the rationale for measuring training is a bit like the ham-trimming ritual. The measurement ritual is based on an unquestioning adherence to the professional assumption and belief that we do it because we're supposed to. Evaluation of training is often performed as some sort of Human Resources and Development (HRD) good-housekeeping practice: ritually prescribed and recommended—although in reality, more talked about than done.

Courageous Training leaders in our experience have confronted the measurement and evaluation assumption head on. They are dissatisfied with current practices and see a lot of wasted and nonproductive effort—a lot of wheel-spinning, but not a lot of forward progress toward valid and useful evaluation results.

In this chapter, we advise all training leaders to seriously question the *what* and *why* of evaluation, challenging the ritualistic but nonproductive practices that tend to be followed. The message that runs through this chapter is quite simple: the goal of training evaluation is *not to prove* the value of training; the goal of evaluation is to *improve* the value of training. More specifically, we suggest how training leaders can take courageous actions on several fronts:

- Rethinking the Kirkpatrick prescription (described below)
- Exposing the false god of return on investment (ROI)
- Confronting the folly of seeking credit
- Telling the truth about training impact (and the lack of it)
- Accurately describing the real causes of training failure
- Getting information to the people who can—and should— do something with it

RETHINKING THE KIRKPATRICK PRESCRIPTION

Virtually all HRD practitioners are familiar with the four-level evaluation framework first articulated by Donald Kirkpatrick in 1957 and written about extensively (Kirkpatrick 1976; Kirkpatrick and Kirkpatrick 2006). Kirkpatrick was a true training evaluation pioneer and made a tremendous contribution to the HRD profession by developing this taxonomy fifty years ago. This hierarchy explains that at the first level we assess learner reactions, learning mastery at the second level, application of learning on the job at the third level, and value to the sponsoring organization at the fourth level. Later, Jack Phillips (2003) added and defined "Level 5" as measurement of the ROI, describing this as the ultimate level of evaluation for training.

Kirkpatrick and Phillips continue their fine work and others build on and refine it. Our Courageous Training colleagues have no quarrel with the general concepts of Kirkpatrick and Phillips. We also appreciate the attention that their work draws to the whole issue of training value and how it should be measured. But we have some serious concerns about their approach.

We have noticed a rampant belief among training practitioners—a belief that Phillips himself has promoted (*Chief Learning Officer Magazine* 2003)—that training departments should follow a suggested formula stipulating the percentage of their efforts that should be subjected to each of Kirkpatrick's four levels of evaluation. According to this guideline, HRD departments would evaluate 100% of their programs on participant-reaction (Level 1), about 60% on learning mastery (Level 2), 30% on behavioral application (Level 3), and 10% or less on impact and ROI (Level 4).

Courageous Training leaders operate with a different perspective. They know that the last thing that should drive which efforts get evaluated and how they are measured is a rote formula, no matter how well-intentioned. The first, final, and only legitimate arbiter of what and how to evaluate is "why"—what purposes are to be served, and why are these purposes important?

We fear that evaluation practitioners often decide which level of evaluation to use in their analyses and studies based principally on which levels of evaluation are easiest and least expensive to do, rather than on the value that can be derived from the information. For example, Level 1, or participant reaction, surveys are indeed easy to design, administer, and analyze. But they are largely superficial in most instances and, in our experience, have virtually no relationship to the amount or relevance of new learning achieved, and even less to do with whether trainees will ever use their learning in on-the-job applications that will yield valuable organizational outcomes.

Courageous Training leaders think carefully about why they need the evaluation data from any of the levels and what decisions the data will help them make. For example, with a new training initiative or with the launch of a new training vehicle, such as podcasts, it may be very important to know how trainees react to it (Level 1) and to collect their opinions for making it easier to use.

Level 2, evaluation of learning, should probably be used in all training programs. First off, feedback is at the heart of learning. Testing for new knowledge helps learners consolidate new knowledge and helps them gauge their mastery so that they can remediate if needed or achieve a sense of satisfaction if they have mastered something new. Test results also help a training leader determine whether more, or less, instruction is needed. In our view, if it's worth teaching in the first place, it's worth knowing if it was learned. So, if any formula is applicable, it ought to be 100% of training gets evaluated at Level 2. Such Level 2 evaluation can take many forms. It may be something that occurs as a formal or separate component at the end of or after the training. It may be something that is less formal (although no less objective) and may well be done as part of the training. The key issue is that both the learner and the organization/facilitator know where the development stands after training.

Return on training investments all comes down to the simple formula we have described in Chapter Three and is driven directly by the number and proportion of trainees who actually apply, on the job, the learning they have acquired from training interventions. It's simple: if they use it (assuming it is worth using in the first place) then it pays off; if they don't, the learning investment is mostly wasted.

So, when it comes to advice on how many learning initiatives ought to be subjected to Level 3 evaluations (i.e., behavioral application), a Courageous Training leader will ask, first, how important it is to the business that trainees actually apply their learning on the job. We have worked with plenty of learning programs wherein the company is "betting the business" on an expectation that the training will actually work. A company that is launching a new product in a new market that could drive a major increase in sales revenues, for example, cannot afford for people to ignore or otherwise not use their new product training. Or, a company that is struggling to attract and retain talent cannot afford for managers to ignore or otherwise not use their new leadership or coaching skills. In cases like these, evaluation should certainly be done to find out who and how many are using their training and who and how many are not. The evaluation should dig deeper into the factors that are enabling application, and those that are impeding on-the-job application. If the need for the training is driven by needs for on-the-job performance change or improvement, then by all means it is worth finding out if this is happening—and if not, why not.

Regarding evaluation beyond Level 3 to assess value to the business and even ROI (Level 5), we come closer to agreeing with the "10% or less" guideline. The real value and impact of training hinges on behavioral application. If people use their training, then ROI and business impact should be a given. If people are not using their training, then lack of business impact and ROI are likewise a given. Since application of learning on the job—aimed at important factors and issues—is the make-or-break linchpin for business impact and value, the greatest evaluation attention should be paid to Level 3—when, how, and why (or why not) are people using their learning? Occasional forays into evaluation beyond this level may be needed for several reasons, such as to gather evidence and examples of the value and impact of learning applications, to support arguments for sustained or increased investment, to defend budgets, to market the training by making claims for its value, and so forth.

EXPOSING THE FALSE GOD OF ROI

The past few years have seen a huge amount of action and anxiety around "proving" the value of training and demonstrating return-on-investment, or, ROI. The original ROI concept is absolutely right-minded and valid: the training must be worth the investment it required. No business can afford to spend money on training that will not return value, and there must be a defensible business rationale for each and every training expense. Courageous Training leaders are especially and wholeheartedly in favor of asking sharply focused ROI questions at the time a training initiative is being proposed.

But pursuit of ROI metrics has taken on a life of its own. For many practitioners it has come to mean that "training should make money" for the business or the corollary assumption that the training with the greatest quantifiable ROI is the best for the business. This is not true. Courageous Training leaders recognize that the goal of training is not to "make money" but to build the capabilities of employees who help the organization make progress toward its business goals and strategies.

Consider this example: A rapidly growing and highly profitable organization is facing a severe talent shortfall and is losing critical employees who are being raided by competitors. To execute its business strategy successfully, this company must do everything in its power to retain its highly skilled and valuable employees. Now imagine that there are two training programs being offered.

Training Program A teaches employees how to identify wasteful activities in their work units and implement revisions that save money. Trainees use their training and make cost-saving changes that lead to an average savings of $4,000 per participant in just the first three months of the year after the training. Audits by the finance department verify that this training achieved an enviable ROI of 400%.

Training Program B teaches supervisors the actions and changes they need for forging better relationships with their employees. Nearly three months after its launch, this expensive program is beginning to work as intended. Supervisors and employees both report a number of improvements, including more open and productive dialogue between employees and managers, the establishment of clearer goals, and an increase in coaching. But after three months, attrition is still occurring—although it has slowed down a bit—and there is no evidence of any other financial outcomes. ROI assessed to date is terrible—a huge net loss.

While both programs have value, Courageous Training leaders will argue that Program B has far more value to the organization than Program A—despite its inferior ROI data—because it is directly addressing a critical need of the organization that, unless successfully resolved, will prevent it from executing its strategy. The ROI data from Program A are impressive, but that result has far less strategic value to the business. However, a misguided training manager obsessed with showing ROI for training might have reached exactly the opposite conclusion. The point? The purpose of training is not to "make money"; it is to support the organization in executing its strategy and achieving its goals. Should it do this at a cost-effective level? Yes, of course, and bold training leaders will always try to trim costs from training processes. But they will also make decisions on the value of training based on the extent to which their results are needed for the business to succeed, not on narrowly conceived estimates of ROI.

Courageous Training leaders, being the business-goal bulldogs that they are, always raise ROI questions at the outset of a training request: Is this training needed for our business? Will it provide the results we need to achieve business success at a cost we can afford? What should we measure to know if the training is providing value? But they avoid the blind pursuit of ROI evidence after the training is completed, as if it were the prized brass ring. They recognize that the real value of results data is in being able to make the connection between training, system performance factors (especially manager behavior), and the business impact. They are not tempted by the false gods of ROI that often lead them to misguided, unnecessary, and self-serving efforts that deflect attention from the real value issue: learning how to get more people to use their training.

CONFRONTING THE FOLLY OF SEEKING CREDIT

As we discussed in Chapter Four, successful training works as a process that stretches far beyond the boundaries of the learning event. Successful training interventions involve several key partners in nontraining roles, especially trainees, managers, and senior executives. If the training works, it works because all of the key players played their parts in the process. If it doesn't work, somewhere a link in the value chain broke. This is the reality of training.

Contrary to this reality, many approaches to evaluation are aimed at parceling out the independent value that can be attributed to the training. The popular ROI processes, for example, include a formulaic calculation for ascribing the proportion of the impact value for which training can take credit.

Savvy training leaders know that training is a fully partner-dependent process; all the partners in the process must do their part to make it work, and it is folly (and self-serving) to try to attribute the lion's share, or any share for that matter, of credit to any single one of the partners. Courageous Training leaders are ready and willing to stand back from the spotlight of praise and to acknowledge the achievements of the partnership. They know, too, that clouding the principal message (i.e., that it takes a partnership to achieve business impact) by attempting to show how much of the credit training should take will come across as naïve, self-serving, or defensive. Furthermore, it will undermine the trust of the partnership that is needed so the training process will continue to work and contribute to the organization's success.

The greatest value from evaluation comes not from *proving* the value of training, but from *improving* the value of training—by discovering what is working and what is not so that changes can be made to drive continuous improvement. Sometimes improving involves proving, as stakeholders need to know what they are getting for their money, time, and energies. In such cases, it is necessary to measure training impact and value. If, for example, an important training investment is not paying off, pointing out the lack of benefit serves to capture the attention of key stakeholders and can allow the training leaders to engage them in a process of problem solving. By the same token, drawing attention to great achievements serves the same purpose, helping all stakeholders notice and appreciate the roles they played and how their actions helped contribute to success.

Sometimes less strategic purposes for evaluation, such as demonstrating participant satisfaction, supporting budget requests, and so forth are needed. Courageous Training leaders will pursue these purposes when they are necessary, but they will never let these tactical efforts supersede or displace evaluation endeavors aimed at improving training effectiveness. Nor will they ever use evaluation to seek credit for training as if it alone were responsible for worthy achievements.

TELLING THE TRUTH ABOUT TRAINING IMPACT AND THE LACK OF IT

Training gets predictable results. There will almost always be some trainees, though proportions may vary, who end up applying their learning in ways that add value. And there will be another proportion who do not use their learning to change or improve performance and for whom training was mostly a waste. For this reason, commonly used evaluation methods that aim to calculate averages will almost always misrepresent the reality of training impact.

The mean or average, as we all know, can be very misleading. If, for example, Bill Gates, Chairman of Microsoft Corporation, were in a room with 1,000 homeless and destitute people, the *average* net worth of those individuals would be about $40 million. But to report that all people in the room are doing well economically would be a deception.

In the same way, it can be dishonest and misleading to report an average impact of training figure, because those few trainees who used their training to accomplish some very valuable results may mask the fact that the larger proportion of trainees got no value at all. The training leader at a member company in our user group, for example, was leading a large and strategically critical training initiative to help managers and directors employ more marketing concepts and tools in their business plans and decision making. They discovered from a study using the Success Case Evaluation Method (Brinkerhoff 2003) that just one of several dozen trainees had used the training to directly increase operating income—an increase of a whopping $1.87 million. It would have been very easy (though our Courageous Training leader from our user group did not succumb to the temptation) to calculate an average impact estimate, which would have made it look as if the typical participant had produced close to $100,000 of value from the training—well above and beyond what it had cost. And indeed, had this training function employed one of the typical ROI methodologies, that is exactly what they would have "discovered" and reported.

Instead, our bold friends in this case happily reported and shared in the recognition for the wonderful success that the training had helped one participant produce. But they also dutifully reported the darker side of the picture, that there was a large proportion of the trainees who got nowhere near this outcome and that many trainees made no use of the training at all. It took courage to tell the whole story, but the truth drew attention to the factors that needed to be better managed in order to get more trainees to use their training in positive ways.

By bringing critical attention to the low-level usage of the training and the projected business consequences that would ensue if the strategic shift could not be made, our user-group friends were able to stimulate key executive decisions in some of the business divisions. These decisions would drive more accountability for employing the new marketing skills and more effective manager involvement. The bold actions of these training leaders spawned a new attention to the many factors that drive impact and enabled the entire organization to accelerate strategic execution more deeply throughout the organization.

Courageous Training leaders always dig beneath the results headline and investigate the causes. Why were these great outcomes achieved? Who did what to cause them to happen? What would it take to get more such outcomes from future training? What prevented other people from getting similar great results? Only when the whole truth about training outcomes is reported, understood, and acted on, can the training function dig itself out of the hole of sustained marginal results for all employees.

ACCURATELY DESCRIBING THE REAL CAUSES OF TRAINING FAILURE

Training can fail for many, many reasons: bad learning design, wrong program for the audience, people attending being unprepared, a mediocre facilitator, people not having an opportunity to try out their learning, people getting training at the wrong time, and so on. Sometimes the failures are for obvious and relatively easily correctable reasons, such as training not being scheduled at times so the right people can get it, when they need it. Other times, the failures are due to more deeply seated and solution-resistant causes. We recall below a case that provides an excellent illustration of this.

Customer Service Training Case Study (or, Who Is Minding the Store?)

Our client—one of the largest computer companies in the world—had offered a two-week residential training program to teach field service technicians how to install, initialize, and troubleshoot upgrades to the huge servers the company sold. This was extremely expensive training that took service technicians out of the field for two weeks and engaged them in practice on a multimillion-dollar simulator. The good news from the evaluation was that the training was very, very effective. We uncovered several instances where service technicians made use of their training in highly critical instances with vital customers—one a major airline, and another one of the world's largest stock exchanges—to avoid computer outages that would have cost many millions of dollars, not to mention a horrific toll on customer satisfaction.

But there was bad news as well. Our evaluation showed that 40% of the trainees never made use of their training, which is a distressingly high proportion especially when the company was receiving an increase in complaints about customer service. With a little digging, we discovered the primary cause of the lack of use: amazingly, the 40% of the trainees who never used their training did not use it for the simple reason that they had no customer—not a single one—that owned or had ordered the equipment that the training program taught technicians to install! Why on Earth, we wondered, would district managers with clients already complaining of lack of service take busy technicians out of the field and send them to an unneeded and expensive residential training program?

The answer lay within some deeply rooted and sensitive political divisions in the company. The district service managers did not trust the sales forecasts that came from the sales leaders, who tended to lowball their forecasts so that they would not be punished if they failed to meet them. So as not to be caught short without a qualified technician when a customer needed to have the new equipment installed, these service managers would send a technician to the training "just in case" a new customer with a service need emerged at the last minute. Because service managers were enrolling technicians on this just-in-case basis, the training course was oversubscribed. There was also a waiting list for participation, sometimes lasting several months. Knowing this, service managers were inclined to enroll several technicians, so they could at least get one into the course, which only made the waiting list even longer. The training department, in the spirit of fairness, enrolled technicians on a first-requested/first-served basis, never knowing that there were many technicians on the waiting list who had no need for the course since they had no customers with the equipment.

By doing an evaluation that looked at the total learning-to-performance process (not just the training program itself), the training leader spotted this issue, understood it, and eventually resolved it. This training leader quite courageously exposed the problem, calculating and reporting the true costs of the 40% failure rate, the lost service capacity, the costs of customer dissatisfaction due to technicians who really did need the training not being able to attend due to the waiting list, and so forth. Armed with this volatile information, the training leader was able to draw the attention of the highest-level senior leaders and engage them in a "summit" meeting to resolve the problems despite their deeply rooted causes.

At several points in our work with this client, there were temptations to simply sweep the problem under the rug. After all, the training manager was not keen on getting in the middle of the forecasting fray between sales and service. And besides, the service technicians who did get the training all enjoyed it and developed great new capabilities. The ROI data on average across the training program was superbly high and made the training department look good—a major boon to help score points in their continuing budget battle. But our bold client refused these temptations, looking at the problem not only from the point of view of the training function but also from a whole-company business perspective, as a true business leader should. From this vantage point, there was no choice but to take bold steps to report the problem truthfully and drive remedial actions, despite the inevitable political fallout that would ensue from rooting out the true causes for failure. This is another case where traditional evaluation methods would not have brought the critical issue to light.

GETTING INFORMATION TO THE PEOPLE WHO CAN—AND SHOULD—DO SOMETHING WITH IT

Most training evaluation models and methods that we encounter are designed and implemented so that the feedback gathered by the training function stays within the training function. A typical Kirkpatrick-based Level 3 practice, for example, is to ask trainees to take a survey some weeks or months after they have been to training. They are asked to report what they are doing or not doing to apply their training. Predictably, most of them are not doing very much with their training. The recipients of this information are the trainers, who (a) already suspect such lack of use is the case, and (b) are the people least able to do anything about the problem. Frequently, however, they are reluctant to share this feedback with line managers or senior managers for fear that it will cast a shadow on the value of the training program and thereby the training department.

In contrast, Courageous Training leaders know that the rightful recipients of Level 3 and other training impact data are the sponsors and customers of training: immediate managers, their bosses, and senior leaders. If good money has been spent giving employees new skills and knowledge that are needed for business success, and these employees are not applying (or are being hindered from applying) their new capabilities on the job, then someone in leadership needs to know. The trick to getting more impact from training is getting the right information to the people who have their hands on the levers that control the factors that keep learning from being used.

Table 6.1 shows clearly that many of the causes for training failure lie in the performance management systems, both formal and informal, that shape employee behavior. From our experience, in almost all cases, the failure of training to achieve maximum possible impact results from the interaction of several possible causes, few if any of which will be within the training department's direct control.

In many cases, actions can be taken by the trainees' immediate supervisors to change these negative factors. Employees who

TABLE 6.1 Common Causes for Training Failure

Cause of Training Failure	Explanation
Level of mastery	Employees did not sufficiently learn or master new knowledge or skills.
Need to learn or apply	Employees may be sent to or otherwise engage in training that is not needed for effective job performance.
Opportunity to apply	Recently trained employees may not encounter opportunities to apply their skills or may not have time because of perceived or real pressures.
Motivation	Employees do not feel as if the training can be helpful to them or see any benefits to be gained from it.
Self-Awareness	Employees do not know what skills they lack or already have or otherwise inaccurately rate their own capabilities; thus they feel they do not need the training.
Feedback	Employees are not aware of the consequences of their performance and/or are not informed about how well (or poorly) they are doing.
Incentives	Employees perceive no actual benefit from applying the learning.
Coaching and mentoring	Employees may try to change their behavior but cannot do it alone without coaching, mentoring, role models, etc.
Direction and expectation	Employees may not know that they are expected to apply the learning or may not sense any accountability for doing so.
Timing	Employees may be engaged in training at an inopportune time that does not align with the greatest need or opportunity to learn and apply it.
Personal capabilities, traits, and attributes	Employees may lack the capability (e.g., experience, language, reading ability) to learn and apply competencies needed for effective performance.

have recently completed training, for example, will typically face competing job responsibilities that may inhibit opportunities to try out new learning. A straightforward step their managers can take is to structure the trainees' post-training work responsibilities so that they have such opportunities, check in with them soon after training, and let them know that they, as their managers, expect their employees to seek opportunities to apply newly learned training.

Sometimes these performance system inhibitors lie beyond the direct influence of immediate managers. For example, incentive and reward systems may not be aligned with the new ways of working that were taught in the training program. All the training in the world cannot lead to changed behavior if, for instance, the new way of working is going to help the employee "earn" a cut in pay. A thorough and objective evaluation process will ferret out such issues. In these cases, the parties responsible for the system inhibitors need to take corrective action.

In still other cases, the training failure culprits are senior leaders who do not set clear expectations and hold their direct reports accountable for supporting the application of training. In yet other instances, the training impact issues are caused by less obvious and culturally rooted procedures, such as the way that training is valued and perceived in the organization. If training is viewed largely as an employee benefit, for example, then there will also be little expectation for training to be actually applied in on-the-job performance.

When Courageous Training leaders give the right line managers and senior executives good evaluation data in a manner that they can understand and use, good things start to happen. One of our user group members reported a wonderful example of senior leaders taking action on training impact data. The company in this case had launched a new sales strategy, part of which included training new sales reps during a residential two-week program on how to sell more profitable and comprehensive systems (versus single products) to customers. Because the training absolutely had to work, the company built in a number of the Four Pillars methods and tools, including an Impact Booster for managers, and one-on-one meetings between district

managers and their reps to help prepare the reps to constructively participate in and apply the training. The training leaders
followed up the launch of the training with a Success Case
Method impact study. The good news they discovered was that
the training, when it was applied, led quickly to an increase of
40% in systems sales—the goal of the training. But the training
was not being applied by reps in nearly one-third of the districts.
The evaluation also looked into which sales managers were doing what to support the training. This inquiry discovered that
in almost every district where there was no large increase in
sales, the district manager had also failed to conduct the before-
training preparation meetings. In the districts where training
application was high and the 40% increase was achieved, district managers had faithfully conducted such meetings. Armed
with the sales impact data, the bottom-line value of the sales
results, what was being spent on the training, and the huge up-
side results that could be achieved with more consistent training
application, the Courageous Training leaders in this company
held a meeting to share the data with the senior vice president in
charge of all sales. Here, briefly, is a dramatic recreation of part of
that meeting, beginning just after the training leaders had walked
the senior vice president through the results:

> SENIOR VICE PRESIDENT: *"Let me see if I have this straight. When
> my district managers conducted these training briefing
> meetings you taught them how to do, we got a 40% increase
> in sales almost 90% of the time. Do I have that right?"*
>
> TRAINING LEADERS: *"Yes, that's right."*
>
> SENIOR VICE PRESIDENT: *"And when they did not hold these
> preparation meetings, their districts almost never got the
> increase?"*
>
> TRAINING LEADERS: *"Yes, that's right too."*

> SENIOR VICE PRESIDENT: *"And, you're telling me that even though you taught them how to do it, almost a third of the district managers are not conducting these meetings?"*
>
> TRAINING LEADERS: *"Yes, that's right again."*
>
> SENIOR VICE PRESIDENT: *"Thanks folks, I'll take it from here!"*

Soon after this meeting, this same senior vice president formulated and mandated a new policy. All new sales reps arriving for the two-week institute would be asked if they and their district manager had engaged in the preparation meeting. If the answer was "no," the training leaders were to politely refuse to admit the reps into the program and were to send them back to the airport, so they could go back to their home districts. It took only one instance of this dramatic action for the district managers to get the message. The company was dead serious about making the new sales strategy work—and equally dead serious that district managers do everything they could to make it, and the training that was vital to its success, work. Subsequent impact evaluation showed a large increase in the number and effectiveness of these pretraining Impact Map discussions and an equally large increase in systems sales across all of the districts. Importantly, the directive to adhere to the training process came not from the training department, where it would have fallen mostly on deaf ears, but from the key stakeholder in the initiative, a senior business leader.

MAKING A BUSINESS CASE FOR IMPROVING TRAINING—THE COURAGEOUS TRAINING EVALUATION STRATEGY

The bold training leaders with whom we have worked follow a relatively simple but profoundly impactful three-step evaluation process called the Success Case Evaluation Method. This process has been described in detail in several other books (Brinkerhoff 2003; Brinkerhoff 2006), so we will not repeat the detailed steps here. But we will provide a general overview of the approach and the type of useful information that it helps Courageous Training leaders uncover. In each step, the training leaders ask a sharply focused set of questions, each set of questions driven by the answers to the questions that preceded them. Then, assuming they have gotten accurate and valid answers to each set of questions, they report their results to the people who can take action, supporting their request for action with a solid business case. Table 6.2 shows the flow of this evaluation process.

This information is collected through a combination of brief surveys and in-depth interviews with participants. Sometimes information is collected from managers or other people who can

TABLE 6.2 Courageous Training Evaluation Process

Step One: Is the training being used?
• Who is using the training, and who is not?
• What parts of the training are being used, and which are not?
• When and where is the training being used, or not used?
Step Two: When the training is used, what good does it do?
• What are the results achieved worth to the business?
• What are the consequences to the business of the training not being used?
• What business value could be achieved by getting the training used more than it currently is?
Step Three: What would it take to get more value from the training?
• What is helping people use the training?
• When the training is not used, why not; what is getting in people's way?
• Can anything be done to get more people using the training, more effectively, more of the time?
• Who would have to do what to get the training used more often, to get more good results?

corroborate the behavior and results. Courageous Training leaders begin the data collection process with a clear idea of the behaviors and business outcomes they are looking for and that matter most to the key stakeholders, and they carefully validate the results to be sure they are verifiable and would "stand up in court."

Sometimes answers to the questions in Table 6.2 imply action needed by the training function itself, such as when the design of the learning experience prevented more people from mastering the learning outcomes, or when training delivery schedules or methods impeded participation. In other cases, and most frequently as we have already noted, the answers to the questions will imply actions needed on the part of nontraining personnel, such as managers of trainees, trainees themselves, Human Resources (HR) systems owners, or senior leaders.

SUMMARY

Courageous Training leaders acknowledge and confront the truth that no training works all of the time. They leverage this reality by dutifully seeking out and accurately reporting the business impact of the training, making sure that all the partners in the training process are fully informed. There is almost always good news to report, and this is communicated accurately, but it is not distorted or misrepresented by, for example, using misleading averages and other statistics that can mask the reality of impact. They make sure that the real causes of training success and failure are dug out and that the responsible parties are fully apprised of who is doing what they need to do in order to make things work better. In doing so, the training leaders continue to respect the commitments they have made to be true partners. By being sure that the people who could be most embarrassed or endangered by evaluation findings are the first to learn about them, the training leaders are careful not to undermine trust and constructiveness.

In summary, the principal actions that operationalize Courageous Training Pillar #4 are as follows:

1. Evaluate the whole learning-to-performance process, focusing on application of the learning.

2. Measure business impact.

3. Investigate the effect of performance system factors.

4. Look specifically at management involvement at all levels.

5. Report the whole truth to the stakeholders; make recommendations for actions to be taken by the persons who have their hands on the levers for change.

6. Follow through with additional evaluation to document and report progress being made, being sure to acknowledge the good work of partners.

7

The Courageous Training Code: Seven Ways to Strengthen Your Leadership Backbone

Courageous Training leaders see themselves as leaders, not administrators, of a training function, though training itself is part of what they do. They also do not see themselves as training vendors, though they do supply training and may bring in training companies to help provide high-quality programs. They do not see themselves as coordinators or brokers of training services, though they do help link people and organizational units with the learning and performance services they need.

Above all, they see themselves as leaders, with responsibilities to the business and the people in it to ensure effective performance and worthwhile results—not just training results but *business* results. Like other leaders in the organization, they are stewards of precious resources, and it is their duty to see that these resources are leveraged into the greatest value possible. Like other leaders in the organization, they have a responsibility to establish and inculcate a vision, to articulate a strategy, to set priorities and goals that reflect the strategy, to ensure effective execution of strategy, and to develop others' skills and talents so that they are maximally successful.

We know from decades of work in the training field that it is easy to fall off the "leadership horse" and succumb to pressures that conspire to devolve the training leadership role into that of a vendor, administrator, or broker of training services. We have seen firsthand how line managers can sometimes treat training staff as if they were simply order takers and delivery people. And we have seen training leaders respond as if the line managers were right.

In this chapter, we introduce and discuss the Courageous Training Code, outlining the mind-sets and principles that guide Courageous Training leaders and help them provide the greatest possible value to those they serve. This chapter is also a prelude to the case examples that begin with Chapter Nine. In these, you will hear directly from four training leaders who have helped drive their organizations to a new level of training value and impact. You will learn from them not only how they employed the concepts and methods of the Four Pillars but also how they followed the Courageous Training Code to help their organizations achieve outstanding results—at the same time beginning a transformation of the way that training is perceived, valued, and executed as a business improvement process.

THE COURAGEOUS TRAINING CODE

The Courageous Training Code is, like the Hippocratic Oath for physicians, a set of principles that is intended to guide conduct and action. Along with the Four Pillars, the code completes the Courageous Training approach. Unlike the Four Pillars, the code does not pertain to methods and tools; it is, instead, a prescription for attitude and belief. While the code ultimately is executed through actions and behaviors, it is not a prescribed method. The code consists of principles that guide behavior for all and any of the circumstances that one will encounter while implementing the methods and tools of the Four Pillars. Here is the code, summarized as a list:

• Decide to be a pioneer

• Think like a business partner, not a training vendor

• Raise customer expectations

• Embrace resistance, don't avoid it

• Negotiate tactics but don't compromise principles

• Be tenacious, don't get deflected

• Share credit, don't seek it

In the following pages, we take each code prescription and expand it with explanations and illustrations of the conduct it is meant to guide.

Decide to Be a Pioneer

At various points in history and on every continent, pioneers have felt a sense of restlessness and dissatisfaction with how things were going in their lives; they held a belief that they could improve their situation. Maybe they were not happy with their current economic situation; maybe they yearned for a better lifestyle with more freedom; or maybe they just wanted a new challenge. No matter what caused the dissatisfaction, at some point they made the bold decision to leave the relative safety, security, and routine of the village where they lived and venture off into the unknown frontier in pursuit of a more rewarding existence. We list "Decide to Be a Pioneer" as the first code because we believe this is the principle that begins the Courageous Training journey. It is a decision to move on and to acknowledge dissatisfaction with the way things are at present.

We draw an analogy between the safe confines of a town and the typical scope of a training department. It is, we think, an apt analogy. The training department has a life inside its walls, and important work is carried out there: planning training events, registering and tracking participants, managing budgets, and so forth. This analogy is not to disparage the vital work that must be accomplished in the department. But it is easy to become insular and caught up in the routine and time pressures of the status quo, thus missing the broader perspective of what is going on outside the department walls and losing sight of the opportunity to really make a difference in how much training actually gets used and the positive impact it can have on an organization.

The first—and fundamental—action that Courageous Training leaders take to begin their journey is to look in the mirror. They ask themselves, being brutally honest, if they like everything they see, and if they are satisfied with how training has been working and what it is producing. Depending on this reflection, they might admit to themselves that although they are providing good training, it is not good enough. They might acknowledge that they are not satisfied with the level of business results that training is producing: that they are paying too much for too little and that too much training is not getting leveraged into improved performance.

In Chapter Ten you will read Dr. Jeff Hafen's account about how his dissatisfaction with his department's ability to clearly measure the impact of their training drove him to relentlessly pursue a better way. Jeff is the Director of Support Staff Training and Development for a megasized school district. Courageous training leaders like Jeff make a decision to take a stand, to do things differently, to take risks if necessary, and to otherwise do what it takes to make training work in their organizations the way it really ought to. They know that things could be better, and they decide that they are the ones who must act—and lead—to make them better. They decide to become pioneers and leave the security of the status quo. They leave the *training* business and get into the business of the business partner.

Think Like a Business Partner, Not a Training Vendor

The training business does need vendors. An organization's training needs and operations have grown so complex and varied that there is no way any training function in today's typical organization could possibly design, plan, and deliver all of the training services it needs to. So we acknowledge: the training world needs vendors, just as the medical profession needs vendors for the dizzying array of drugs, devices, and tools that are available in the ever-growing healthcare industry. The vendor's role is to represent its product, show the value of the product in solving the serious problems of prospective clients, and help those clients make a wise purchase decision.

But just as we would not want a pharmaceutical sales representative as our personal physician or managing our total health needs, organizations should not want their training leaders to play the role of training vendor. The anecdote recalled below helps demonstrate why a training leader should not focus on being a training vendor.

A few years back, one of the authors was a Vice President for a large training company and was invited to meet with the Training Director at a Fortune 100 company's division headquarters. Hoping this prestigious company could benefit from some of our training solutions, the conversation started by trying to uncover the business needs that the potential client was facing to better gauge if any of our programs might address those needs. After several attempts to uncover issues, it became apparent that this training director was not really familiar with (maybe even unaware of) the business challenges of his division. All the questions were pretty much answered with a response similar to: "I am not really sure if we have those issues, but I think we're OK there."

After several minutes of this type of exchange, and obvious frustration on both sides, I asked, "If you're not really certain about the business needs of your company, why did you invite us here to meet with you?" His response cleared it all up. "You see," he said, "I am responsible for publishing the company training catalog." He proudly pulled out the current year's catalog and explained how the offerings were categorized by topic, by audience level, and by training need. He showed how the various programs were linked to the company's competencies and, flipping pages back and forth, showed that the topics were cross-referenced. He spoke in detail about the best sellers in each content area and rattled off statistics about the number of hours spent in training per employee, cost per training hour, ratio of classroom to e-learning offerings, and so forth. Eventually, he explained that workshop enrollments had been declining over the past few years and it was his job to get them moving again. Then he paused—either because he forgot where he was heading with all this or so everyone could adequately savor the full extent of his catalog masterpiece—leaned back in his chair, and said: "So what I need are some fresh programs that are really exciting and will really draw participants in. Do you have any of those? And what can you do to help us do a better job of marketing them internally?" Clearly, here was a training leader who was taking his organization in the wrong direction, thinking like a training vendor not a business partner.

Training leaders who operate from a vendor mentality will see their responsibility as selling as much training as they can. They will want to be sure that the organization has a fully stocked cupboard of programs and tools. They will want to be sure that that supply gets used, that training enrollments grow, that training classes run—like a good hotel—with a high occupancy rate. They will often operate by the *law of the hammer* such that every problem they encounter looks more and more like a nail. As Pat in our opening story in Chapter Two could have done (but chose not to), they will jump on every expressed request or inquiry to build it into the largest sale of training services possible. Given budget and accountability realities and common customer expectations, it is difficult for training leaders not to behave like salespeople. As we have pointed out, training department metrics often focus on numbers of training hours delivered, number of people trained, or some other dubious measure of productive value. Selling as much training as possible will help one look good against the metrics.

Training leaders who adopt a business partner mentality, however, will see requests for service as expressions of dissatisfaction with the way things are or as a need for change. Their first and foremost action will be to learn more about the problem and why it is important to the client. They will see their primary and overarching responsibility as helping the client achieve business goals, all within the context of the larger organization's purpose and strategy. They will provide training if and when it is needed, but only in a way that will drive the optimal business results (and not just training results).

Raise Customer Expectations

We frequently make presentations to senior executives and line managers about the High Impact Learning (HIL) approach during which we routinely ask the audience this question: "Based on your experience how much training do you believe actually sticks and gets applied back on the job and leads to business impact?" Without fail the answers we hear from these customers of training are estimates ranging from 5% to 20%. It doesn't matter whether we are addressing a management team comprised of sales, engineering, marketing, operations, or technology leaders, the answer is very consistent; it is always in this very mediocre range. Though most audience members make estimates based simply on their own experience, their "guesstimates" sadly are borne out by previous research and our broad evaluation experience.

We have had conversations with some training managers who, although they agree with the statistics, are threatened by this data. They have said they would never consider sharing this information with their senior management, because they don't want to draw attention to the failings of training for fear that their budgets will be cut—or worse yet, they themselves fired! Other training managers are content with this level of expectation. After all, if this is the typical range of results, then keeping expectations where they are is staying in safe territory.

In contrast, Courageous Training leaders do not want to hide these facts hoping that senior management won't notice or will be so busy with bigger problems that they will ignore the training's shortcomings. Unlike the school children without their homework assignment completed who don't dare make eye contact with the teacher for fear they will be called upon, these bold training leaders recognize this as an opportunity to make a difference and change how the game is played. They are not afraid to speak out about the excessive scrap rate from training and the root causes of this problem. They correctly view this as the perfect chance to raise the organization's expectations for what level of results it should be getting from training and development. They look for the chance to stand up and say to senior management: "Are you happy with these results? Because I'm not satisfied. I am embarrassed by the return we are getting for our training investments, and I know we can do much better. The organization deserves better. And with your help I am convinced we can change these results dramatically and double or triple the return we get for our efforts and investments. Are you in?" Not only will they not satisfice and tolerate minimally acceptable results as being good enough for themselves, but they refuse to let their customers satisfice when it comes to training results.

Courageous training leaders seek to raise the expectations for all key stakeholders so there is no turning back—for the business or for themselves. They want the organization to expect and demand great results from training investments, even if it means holding the training department to higher standards. By the same token they continuously and relentlessly educate stakeholders through discussions, through the development of Impact Maps, and through the presentation of Success Case evaluation reports on what expectations for supporting actions must be set for all stakeholders (especially senior leaders, managers of trainees, training professionals, and trainees) in order for training interventions to produce those lofty results.

Larry Mohl, Vice President and Chief Learning Officer at Children's Healthcare of Atlanta (whose story you'll read in Chapter Nine) went out on an unusual limb in raising expectations. He made the bold decision to not pursue full multiyear funding for the executive development program up front. Instead he welcomed the challenge of having to report on and prove the value of the program one year at a time, and he suggested that funding reapproval be based on evidence of the extent to which their leadership development program produced worthwhile business results. While some of our colleagues thought Larry had lost his sanity, his daring action to raise expectations put him on an equal footing with other *business operations* in this vast healthcare organization, and as a result, earned even greater attention and commitment from senior leaders.

An organization with high expectations for training is an organization that is moving down the path toward becoming a true learning organization. This is part of the Courageous Training leader's long-term strategy. The Courageous Training leader captures every opportunity and interaction to send the message: Training should work for almost all of our employees almost all of the time to help achieve worthy business results. And none of us should rest until it does!

Embrace Resistance, Don't Avoid It

If you are not getting resistance you are probably not working to change the right things. Being a pioneer and implementing the methods and tools of the Four Pillars is leading a change process. It is not just putting on another training program with a few new components. Implementing the methods and tools of the pillars changes the paradigm for training; it shifts the responsibility for achieving results from just the training department to other key stakeholders. As is the case with all valuable organizational change efforts, there will be resistance. This new way of doing training asks the internal stakeholders to change their behaviors and do things differently to ensure the training will actually be used back on the job and lead to important business results. These requests will be hard for stakeholders who do not fully understand the need for change to accept. They will want the results of the change, but they may resist the change in process required to get there. As a result they will demonstrate some resistance and push back on the proposed steps during the process. If they do not resist at all, then chances are they either do not understand the demands this new way of making training work will place on them, or they do understand and are planning to ignore the additional responsibilities.

Courageous Training leaders expect some resistance and do not despair. They recognize that the line on the graph of progress is not a straight line that ascends from low to high. The line of progress will definitely ascend from low to high over time, but it will have peaks, and dips, and then new peaks. Courageous Training leaders are prepared for this roller-coaster ride, recognize that it is part of the natural process, and press forward when they hit these dips. It is tempting to try to avoid resistance and to back away when one encounters it—that's human nature. It is also very dangerous in a change process, because avoiding resistance creates a "false positive" perspective. The leader of a change initiative who never encounters any resistance is not really creating any change.

Negotiate Tactics but Don't Compromise Principles

If there is one prediction about Courageous Training work that we can make with great certainty it is this: try it, and you will be met with suggestion after suggestion that you make less demanding requests for cooperation and involvement from non-training elements in the organization. When we first raise the topics of conducting Impact Boosters (where managers learn what they can do to help ensure that training works for their employees), what we often hear is this lament: "You have got to be kidding me. We can hardly get our managers to give up their time to go to any training. Now you want them to go to training *about* training?" We can almost promise you that if you suggest that managers need three hours for an Impact Booster, you will get a suggestion back that maybe the most time they could ever give, and that is only maybe, is thirty minutes.

Because the Impact Booster approach is new and requires some extra work on the part of managers, it almost always gets some resistance. When meeting resistance (or even just anticipating resistance), it is tempting for the change leaders to avoid pushing for managers to participate in an Impact Booster session. The stakeholder may say, "We don't have time for this, because the managers are too busy. Just send the Impact Map out to the workshop participants."

Courageous Training leaders recognize this request for what it is—a disaster waiting to happen. Although sending out the Impact Map to the participants would enable them to avoid the conflict with the senior stakeholder and give them a warm feeling that they are taking action to keep the process moving, in the long run it will undermine the process and significantly reduce the extent to which the training initiative will lead to business results. Avoiding this resistance (and gaining the temporary good feeling of eliminating a conflict with a senior stakeholder) is really a false positive and misleads the training professional that all is well, when, in fact, they have only postponed the train derailment. Members of our user group have successfully addressed this issue by meeting the resistance head on, and exploring where it's coming from. They understand the *why* behind the resistance and the need for identifying and negotiating tactical changes that will overcome the objections without compromising the principles. They have creatively developed a half dozen alternatives, from classroom sessions to web-based seminars, even individual telephone calls if that is all that will work. Julie Dervin's story in Chapter Twelve provides an excellent example of a Courageous Training leader taking a principled stand on this critical issue. Julie is the Vice President of Learning and Development for Insight Enterprises.

Be Tenacious, Don't Get Deflected

All of the training leaders in our user group have two things in common. First, they have all accomplished some significant gains in training effectiveness and business results for their organizations. This is why they are in the group in the first place. Second, they have admitted in informal discussions with us, that they have faced times and instances where their personal will was tested and they were tempted to give up on employing the methods and tools that comprise the Four Pillars. We had exposed them to the HIL methods and tools that comprise the Four Pillars; we had taught them how to apply the methods, through workshops we conducted with them and through the side-by-side consultation with them that followed our engagements. It was not until later that they in turn taught us. What we learned from them was that making the methods and tools work was not a straight-line path nor was it free of bedeviling obstacles.

As the other principles of the Courageous Training Code imply, the journey of implementing the Four Pillars is not driven on a smooth four-lane highway. It is a more arduous uphill road; and while it is not impossible to traverse (as their achievements testify), it is a road that has many exit opportunities. When managers resist participation in Impact Booster sessions, when senior leaders pull back from holding managers accountable for supporting their trainees, when trainees balk at making specific commitments to actions to apply their learning, and when the other obstacles and issues are confronted, they sometimes seem overwhelming and the journey looks too difficult. These temptations to divert from the path can be great. In Chapter

Eleven, Lisa Bell (Manager of Holcim's North American Learning Center) talks of times when the senior executives from various business units suggested to her that perhaps the expectations for producing concrete business results from the leadership development initiative were indeed too high. More than once, it was tempting to lower expectations for the program and avoid all the frustration. But Lisa and the other courageous leaders we know acknowledged their temptations, momentarily considered them, then reflected yet again on the principles that mattered to them; they persisted in their pursuit of higher and more worthy outcomes.

We considered not even including this tenacity principle in the code, as perhaps it is too obvious. But we opted on the side of inclusion, and we did so because including this prescription serves as a forewarning. It says to expect obstacles, to be prepared to divert from initial plans and make compromises on tactics, and above all, to be ready to be tempted to give up and lower your expectations. Expect the temptation to quit, but make a commitment to stay the course. The goal of doubling or tripling business results is indeed possible, and well worth the pursuit.

Share Credit, Don't Seek It

Throughout this book we have made the following key points: Training alone never produces results. Getting training to produce results is a whole-organization responsibility. When training does work, it works because a host of players and factors were aligned to make it work. And when training does not work, these players and factors were not aligned—or the players did not take the necessary actions.

Courageous Training leaders hold these beliefs close to the heart. Each of them recognizes that he or she is the maestro for the symphony of change. As the maestro, the leader plays a critical role in producing a good performance and yielding good results. However, the leader also recognizes that the maestro alone cannot produce the results, so Courageous Training leaders look for ways to publicize how the *entire process* is working and how the various players (stakeholders) are enabling it to work. They never try to seek the credit for themselves or the training department alone; they always aim to share credit and consistently communicate the message that results are a team effort for which no one individual can take credit.

We believe that most training professionals are not so self-serving that they would seek to take *all* the credit for success when training works. But there are concepts and tools frequently used by training professionals that belie the "share credit" principle. Several return on investment (ROI) evaluation methodologies that are currently popular among the training profession attempt to parcel out the degree or percentage of a positive outcome that can be attributed to the training alone. Even if it were methodologically possible to do this in any definitive way (which it is not), trying to arrive at a training-alone estimate is just bad strategy. First, it flies in the face of the reality that business results require a systemic performance improvement process that involves several factors—not just training. Second, data that attempt to estimate training's causal contribution are likely to be viewed by senior or line managers as self-serving, lacking credibility, and naïve. Third, it will inevitably undermine the hard work done to build bridges to the nontraining partners. Better to leave it alone.

The principle of sharing credit applies not only to how and why training leaders pursue evaluation and measurement but also to how they comport themselves in all interactions with stakeholders. The attitude from the first interaction to the last, and all in between, should be one of equal partner: a business colleague with some special expertise and talents to lend, for sure, but also a person who knows that no one party or role can accomplish the goals that Courageous Training targets.

SUMMARY

The members of our user group who have successfully implemented the Courageous Training process helped us formulate the Courageous Training Code. They didn't help us formulate the code by *telling* us the practices; they helped us create the code through the instinctive behaviors and highly successful actions they took in their projects. Watching them work, talking to them about their actions, and analyzing their successes for how they accomplished things helped us codify these high-leverage practices.

For most people who start on the journey, the prescriptions of the Courageous Training Code begin as specific, planned, and purposeful actions they try to take in their implementations. As they gain more experience in the process, training leaders will internalize these practices. The code will eventually become part of the leaders' unconscious repertoire, their philosophy, and how they view the world.

8

Introducing Four Courageous Training Leaders

The path from business-as-usual training to training that makes a worthwhile difference to the business is a long, up-hill, and rocky road. We are honored to work with many training leaders from our user group who have forgone the opportunities to exit for an easier route and have achieved some remarkable results for their organizations and the employees in them.

Four of these bold leaders tell their stories in the following chapters. We wish that length limitations could have permitted us to include more such stories, as it was difficult to cull only four from the potential pool of Courageous Training profiles. But the four we chose represent an excellent range of industries, approaches, and challenges faced.

All of the authors who wrote case examples refer to a similar set of methods and tools with which readers may not be familiar, because they are part of proprietary training approach called the Advantage Way system. Each of the four authors is a member of the Advantage Way User Group, sponsored by Advantage Performance Group (APG). The Advantage Way system is APG's proprietary version of High Impact Learning (HIL)—the conceptual framework, methods, and tools developed initially by Robert O. Brinkerhoff (see Brinkerhoff and Apking 2001) and continuously upgraded and refined. The system helps training leaders plan and design learning interventions that are guaranteed to help participants achieve increased business impact. The Resources section at the end of this book provides an explanation of the tools and terms referred to in the four case examples. Brief summaries of each of these four stories follow below, highlighting the type of industry in which each courageous leader works and, more importantly, the principal sort of challenge each leader faced that demanded bold action.

Children's Healthcare of Atlanta

Larry Mohl, Vice President and Chief Learning Officer at Children's Healthcare of Atlanta, works in the fast-growing and complex world of health care, bringing experience in training leadership from Motorola and more recently American Express. Larry's challenge was to create a highly effective executive leadership program where rapid growth created a vital need for an expanding pool of highly capable leaders. While Larry was blessed with exceptionally supportive senior leadership, the challenges he faced and the vital needs of the business tested all of his considerable training expertise and leadership skills. He foresaw that the organization might take executive education for granted, view it as just another expense in the budget, and eventually lose executive interest and support for the effort.

Larry had to ensure that the executive education program was being viewed as a strategic investment for the long-term success of the organization, and not just another line item in the budget. He and his team deftly met this challenge by achieving and thoroughly documenting some of the most outstanding business results (operational, financial, and clinical) for a leadership development program that any of us in the training world have seen, or are likely to see.

Clark County Public Schools

Dr. Jeff Hafen, Director of Support Staff Training and Development, leads all staff training in the Clark County (Las Vegas, Nevada) public schools, a huge district with phenomenal growth. For the past three years, the district has built and added a new school each month. Jeff and his team, charged with training all the new staff being brought onboard, faced massive delivery challenges that would intimidate even the most seasoned professionals. No one would have blamed Jeff's group for simply looking past the complex quality and effectiveness issues for the time being and just buckling down to the challenge of delivering the massive number of hours of training that the district needed.

But Jeff looked beyond the sheer delivery challenge to raise the question: What if we provided all of this training but it didn't work? The training was essential for the public good— new staff had to perform well or the district's children and the other constituents would suffer. Thus Jeff led a mission to convert the way that the district conceived of and implemented its training programs to employ all aspects of the Four Pillars. Effecting this type of change in a large public and bureaucratic organization is not easy. His challenge was akin to trying to turn a cruise ship. It doesn't happen easily or quickly, but by taking the helm and steering a steady course for a period of time, a skilled helmsman can change the direction of the vessel.

Holcim

Holcim is one of the world's leading suppliers of cement and aggregates (crushed stone, sand, and gravel) as well as ready-mix concrete and asphalt products and services. Active in more than seventy countries and employing some 90,000 people, the company has a mission to be the world's most respected and attractive company in the industry. Lisa Bell, Manager of the North American Learning Center, was hired to help Holcim institute a centralized learning function that would serve all of the company's United States and Canadian operations.

Lisa's challenge was to make this brand-new centralized learning function work, building a reputation for delivering business value, not just popular training programs. An exceptional aspect of Lisa's work is that she was able to meet leadership's requests for "soft skill" programs but at the same time directly link the training to compelling business metrics that her constituents readily bought into. She steadfastly worked to raise the expectations of the organization and her internal customers to ensure that training investments were truly investments in important business results, such as safety improvements, operations efficiency, and financial performance.

Insight Enterprises

Julie Dervin is Vice President of Learning and Development at Insight Enterprises, a rapidly growing information technologies (IT) solutions provider. Like others in its industry, Insight was seeking to change its value proposition and become a preferred solution-providing "partner" to its customers. Julie led the sales training initiative that supported this transformation. Previous to this strategic shift, training was alive and relatively well at Insight but was mostly a tactical activity that ebbed and flowed based on the whims of managers, always taking a backseat to budget cuts and time pressures. Because training was viewed entirely as the responsibility of the training department, Julie's unit was in the classic bind of being viewed as an order-taking and delivery function.

Julie's challenge was getting the executive and managerial alignment and commitment to supporting actions—not just lip service and permission for people to attend training—and then holding people accountable for applying their learning and changing their sales behaviors. She embraced the HIL principles and had the courage to press forward, ensuring a new breed of training with clear and vital roles for managers of trainees, senior leaders, and others. Her story takes the reader through her trials and travails on this journey, sharing the bold actions she and others took to transform the training operations and culture at Insight.

In the case study chapters, text boxes highlight how these four leaders used the Courageous Training Model.

9

Case Example #1: Diary of a CLO

Executive Development at Children's Healthcare of Atlanta

LARRY MOHL
Vice President and Chief Learning Officer

Wednesday, November 29, 2006

It's 2 a.m. and I can't sleep. At 9 a.m. tomorrow morning we are presenting the results from our first year of the Center for Leadership to our CEO and the senior leadership team. Continued funding for the program is decided by our Board of Directors based largely on the recommendation from the senior team. Is our story compelling enough to warrant continued funding?

We have collected what we feel is solid performance improvement and business impact information from our first graduating class to show we are on the right track. The senior team has been very supportive and involved in the program. They have

139

placed a lot of trust in us and have invested significantly in this initiative. We certainly don't want to let them or the organization down. Has the program delivered enough impact? The funding in the first year has allowed us to build the program from scratch and hire the people we need to support it over the long term. Did I pick up my suit from the cleaners?

Being the Chief Learning Officer (CLO) at Children's Healthcare of Atlanta has been a dream come true. I really enjoyed the senior learning and organization development roles I had at Motorola, and being the CLO at American Express was a great experience. Moving into health care and coming to Children's two years ago has been rewarding in countless ways. Children's Healthcare of Atlanta is an organization that truly "gets it" when it comes to the importance of people and development. I'll never forget my first interview with our CEO, James E. Tally, Ph.D., back in September of 2004. He asked that if I came onboard, would it be all right if he still called *himself* the Chief Learning Officer. I laughed and said I would have to think about it. Yeah, right. It didn't take long after I joined the organization to understand these were not just words. His strong support of learning and desire to create "an adult schoolhouse" at Children's had led him to create a CLO position long before it was fashionable in health care. This focus had earned Children's recognition as a Training Top 100 learning organization for three straight years at the time I joined.

The rest of the senior team understands the need to grow talent internally and is actively involved in that pursuit. Under the leadership of Linda Matzigkeit, our Senior Vice President of Human Resources, the organization has arrived on the Fortune list of the 100 Best Companies to work for in America. We even exceeded our own expectations when we were recognized as one

of the top children's hospitals in the nation by *Child Magazine*—
ahead of when we thought it possible.

Yet even with this high level of senior leadership belief and the
depth of experience I brought to the job, building an effective
leadership development initiative poses significant challenges.
Conducting development as a business improvement process
rather than just a series of educational events entails demands
on the time and attention of all of
the leaders, not just the learning department staff. There were times
when making it all work was an up-
hill struggle for everyone, and even
the most committed and farsighted
CLO would be tempted to take the
easy route: bring in a few leadership
gurus; thrill the participants with a

> Larry decides to be a
> pioneer, recognizing a new
> course of action is needed;
> the safe route will not
> deliver the necessary
> results.

dramatic agenda; and go for the gold of rave reviews, forgetting
about really trying to change behavior and culture. When I look
back at my diary over the past two years it's amazing to see the
twists and turns on our journey to make the Center for Leadership a reality. I'm glad I took the time to keep this diary starting
back in October of 2004.

Monday, October 24, 2004

The Atlanta metro area is one of the fastest growing in the nation. The need for pediatric health care is projected to grow
significantly beyond our capacity to deliver our mission of providing excellence in patient care, integrated research and teaching, and advocating for children. Working with the state, we
were granted a certificate of need for the largest hospital building expansion in the history of Georgia. Staring into an expanded

and more complex future, our Board of Directors has realized that the organization was going to have a tremendous leadership gap. It's not going to be enough for our leaders to manage the current operation. Our leaders are going to have to drive significant change in the way the system delivers care.

I'm encouraged that Linda, Senior Vice President of Human Resources, had already paved the way in helping the rest of the senior team and board see what the future could be like if we did nothing about our leadership issue. I am even more encouraged by how the senior team and board responded. The *Webster's* definition of courage is "the quality of being fearless or brave; valor; pluck." Calling for the development of the Children's Center for Leadership and backing it up with a substantial investment of funds was a pretty plucky move. Especially since the corporate landscape is not exactly crowded with examples of organizations that have moved the needle on this issue in a sustainable way. Starting the process is relatively easy. Sustaining the effort and investment to actually deliver the results is the harder part. I wonder if our senior team really understands what it's getting itself into. Are we courageous enough to stay the course?

Thursday, January 27, 2005
We presented our Center for Leadership architecture today to our senior team. In the past, Children's, like many healthcare organizations, was sending its leaders off to external leadership development programs. While many of these programs are excellent, the cost to send people to them and the lack of practical application of the learned theories back on the job makes that approach insufficient. This is not going to work for us. We need to equip current leaders to meet their increasing challenges, establish a consistent pipeline of leaders for the future, and establish Children's as a great place for leaders to lead. In order to accomplish

these goals we need a holistic approach that links together leadership learning, succession planning, and talent management. We need a language of leadership supported by methods and tools that everyone uses. We need to create tiers of development that help leaders grow from the bottom up. We need leaders to act

> Larry begins to raise the expectations of the organization for what it should be getting from its investment in executive development and what it will take to make this happen.

as faculty, make sure that participants' managers get actively involved, and measure the results of what we are doing in tangible terms. Wow, can't we just send people to some training?

It's been several months now since we got started doing the background work to develop the Center for Leadership. Sometimes it's difficult to realize that all the hard work so far has basically resulted only in alignment on why and how we want to proceed. But while it seems like slow going, I know from past experience that if we don't take the time to set this up right, it will be tough to keep it on track. I give our senior team a lot of credit for taking the time to work through the full approach, asking

> Larry and his team work as partners with the senior management to clarify the business goals and to avoid the temptation of rushing to deliver training.

tough questions, and helping to think things through.

One of the best things that came from today's meeting was that we agreed to "learn our way forward." While we are using many best practices from our experience and research on other companies, we have never done this at Children's before. I wish everything could be perfectly figured out before we enroll our first class, but that would be a fool's journey. It will serve us better if we build a strong evaluation component into our design, look closely and critically at our progress, share the good news as well as the bad, and learn from our emerging experience.

Wednesday, April 13, 2005

Tomorrow we have an important check-in meeting with the senior team. We have designed the Center for Leadership Executive Experience so that it is significantly more than just a single "event." We are fully committed to designing and implementing this development as a High Impact Learning (HIL) process, with heavy investments in creating focus and alignment across all levels of leadership, engaging learning activities that focus on skill and practice, and intensive follow-up to sustain learning and application. As we've envisioned it, the experience combines assessment, workshops, action learning projects, coaching, and follow-through management.

We had previously discussed how the senior team should be involved and decided that they should go through much of the experience prior to other participants. Participating would help them understand what others will be learning, adopt the language, and be better coaches. It is going to be a significant investment of their time and we want to make sure the experience is a positive one. It was relatively easy during the early design stages to get all the stakeholders to agree to the concept of engagement and support from everyone.

But we are all learning as we proceed that delivering on that commitment takes real time and energy—a scarce commodity in an already busy environment.

Thursday, April 25, 2005

What a meeting today!

After some discussion it became apparent that there was some uneasiness in the room. I guess it would have been easier to just let it ride and hope it wasn't anything significant. No one was saying out loud that they were concerned, but concern was hanging in the air. I decided to put it on the table. As I questioned and probed deeper, people expressed serious concerns about how this leadership development experience will play out for their people. The time, energy, and focus required are more than they had imagined. A number of questions were raised, all good ones, but sure to set the stomach acid churning: Maybe we didn't fully understand what we were signing the organization up for. We are in one of the most intense periods in the history of the organization. Can busy people dedicate themselves to this?

> Larry goes beyond embracing resistance; he actually solicits it because he knows it is there beneath the surface.

This was a moment of truth in the making. It was rapid fire from there. Idea, question, benchmark company example, concerns, more ideas, solutions. There are certain core principles that make any development approach work, but there are also areas of flexibility. Keeping these in mind, I helped the group clarify and arrive at decisions about where we need to hold firm on the approach, even if it demands more from us, and where we can flex. One issue that put us to the test today was physician involvement. Developing physician leadership is very important to us and we had made the decision that physicians should go through exactly the same experience as everyone else. Being in a cohort with nonphysicians would build new relationships and perspectives for everyone involved. This is different from how anyone else was doing it,

> Tactics and details are negotiated, but the principles of what it will take to deliver the results are never compromised.

as most organizations had separate programs for physicians. The practical reality is that physicians wear multiple hats that may involve clinical, research, teaching, and administrative responsibilities, leaving limited time for the type of robust experience embodied in the Center for Leadership. Through a facilitated discussion we confirmed that we needed to stay firm on bringing diverse groups together and we would tailor each physician's involvement in projects and other activities outside core workshops to work with the demands of their role.

As I reflect on the meeting I think the most important thing we accomplished today was to set the tone for how we can work through future challenges that can, and will, arise. We came up with some important improvements today. We kept true to the core program intent, and I could see the level of recommitment rise by the end of the meeting.

Tuesday, June 25, 2005

There is no turning back now. We launched our first workshop for our first full class today. Fourteen leaders have been selected through our talent review process. Their Center for Leadership experience will last about sixteen months. They were all briefed and have gone through our assessment center, but I can only assume that they don't really understand what they have signed up for. How could they? As I stood up in front of these folks to introduce our first workshop, Personal Mastery and Change Leadership, I felt excited, apprehensive, honored, and an overwhelming feeling of responsibility. We have rallied the organization, committed key leaders as sponsors and participants, and spent precious resources. But a number of questions nagged in the back of my mind: Is it going to work? Is it a good idea to have physician, clinical, and administrative leaders going through the program together? Will it work for leaders with lots of experience as well as relatively new leaders? Maybe we should have hired a few "rock star" professors? Will anyone actually use the concepts and tools we are teaching?

Monday, September 19, 2005

I attended two meetings today that illustrated the yin and the yang of our progress so far. In the first meeting, a Center for Leadership participant was discussing a change she was driving. I was heartened when she took out one of the tools they had learned to use in our workshop on Personal Mastery and Change Leadership. "Yes!" I thought to myself. Here it is in the "real world." I walked out of the meeting feeling pretty good. In the second meeting one of our participants was leading a meeting on a shift in his strategy. I kept thinking that at some point he would unveil the models he learned, but it just didn't happen without some prompting. We need to find even better ways to help participants connect the dots between what they are learning in the Center for Leadership and the challenges sitting right in front of them every day.

Wednesday, September 21, 2005

I spoke with my team today about my observations from a few days ago. We determined that our team could divide and conquer to increase our support of the action learning projects that had just been launched. While we couldn't follow each participant around to every meeting, the structure of projects would give us an opportunity to insert ourselves to drive reflection and connection to Center for Leadership methods and tools. We decided to include more time in each workshop to discuss insights and actions from past learning and we decided to create an application guide. The guide will be sent to the participants' managers with a request to discuss what their participants are learning and applying as well as tips for how to best support the creation of impact. Finally, we decided to investigate automated systems that could help keep the Center for Leadership content and participants' development goals top of mind.

Friday, January 13, 2006

Action learning. I have a love, hate relationship with action learning. We designed action learning into the experience and it was absolutely the right thing to do, since people learn best and most deeply from action and engagement. But it is difficult to make action learning work for the people involved and the organization at the same time. To work right, action learning projects have to be real projects with results that will be valued. They can't be "make work" or no one takes them seriously. But when they are real and vital, then too often the "action" portion takes over and displaces attention to learning. Many times action learning turns out to be action *or* learning instead of action *and* learning. Great results are achieved but no one learns anything new; or interesting white papers are written with no real impact.

We are determined to get the balance right. It has been a bumpy road and this is one area where we are definitely learning our way forward.

I am keenly aware of the risks involved in this "learning it forward" approach. It could easily backfire if the bumps and potholes we are sure to encounter are seen as failures of the CLO and the learning function staff. This is part of what wakes me up and keeps me up in early morning encounters with myself. These are the times when I have to lean again on the foundation of belief that this approach is really the only way to get real change and impact to happen. I have to trust in our concept that making leadership development work is really a whole-organization process and responsibility, that setbacks are an inevitable part of learning, and that the evaluative feedback we gather—the good and the bad—is just what we need to keep this process continually improving.

Tuesday, August 1, 2006

To get a solid assessment of the business impact and value of our leadership development initiative, we used the Success Case Evaluation Method. Today we started our success case interviews. It's time to answer all the questions we had when we started and to find out, in a systematic way, how the program is truly working. Yes, our funding depends on demonstrated value, but at our core, we feel a responsibility to find out. All of us in this leadership development venture are in it for the long run. We are not just trying to make this work once, and then move on to something else. Our plan and the organizations' need are for a long

> Larry's team strategically uses evaluation to provide the organization with candid feedback to "learn forward" on what parts of the process are working and which parts need improvement.

term and continuing leadership development process that really works. For those of us in Human Resources (HR) who have been involved in efforts where we did not, or could not, see the impact of our efforts, it is terribly troubling. This time, we all agree, we need to see the results we are achieving when this works, and confront the lost opportunities when it does not.

We turned to the success case approach as our method of choice largely because the underlying measurement philosophy matched our philosophy of how learning turns into performance. The statement that stuck with us when we were trained by Dr. Rob Brinkerhoff was "it's not how good the training is, it's how well the organization uses the training." We feel we have designed the Center for Leadership experience for impact right from the start. The buzz on the program is good, but that is just not good enough. We need credible specifics that show the impact so far and the areas for improvement.

Friday, August 18, 2006
I'm starting to get excited. We have completed ten success case interviews and so far the impact has been palpable. People are telling us about impact on them personally and how they lead their part of the operation. Some of the operational improvements they have driven have real financial impact. It's taken a lot of time and energy to bring out the financial component in all of this. I'm grateful that we have had our partners from finance working on this with us. It's very important that we use "Children's-speak" when we talk about the Center for Leadership impact, especially when addressing financial impact. We want to make sure that when all is said and done we have results that the senior executives truly believe because they are tangible and see as relevant because they deal with issues important to our system. We don't want to report statistics that Human Resources and Development (HRD) professionals would be impressed by, but seem academic or meaningless to senior executives.

Monday, September 4, 2006
I've been thinking about how we can help our senior team, the participants themselves, and the larger organization visualize the value that is being created by this first Center for Leadership class. With all the impact our participants are having, it would be absolutely horrible if we can't present the story in a compelling way. Packaging is important, and I need to think carefully about my audiences and what will connect with them.

Wednesday, September 13, 2006
Over the years I have learned that people need to see both a rational and emotional connection to something if they are to be

convinced it is valuable. We are in the process of designing our last workshop called Leadership Next, and this simple principle gave me an idea. Leadership Next is being designed so that participants can reflect on what they have learned and what is next for them in their leadership journey. We can create a big spreadsheet that has a row for each participant and a column for each of the twenty-five Center for Leadership concepts. We can develop a concept card for each specific concept that gives a refresher visual, as well as tips for putting the concept into action. The participants could then do a card sort, picking the concepts that they have put into action and concepts that they want to work on next. Each person can put an "O" in each cell where they have successfully driven application and an "N" in each cell where they want to focus next. Voila! This simple visual will show patterns of application and areas of future focus. I imagine it would look something like Table 9.1 (on the next page).

Because we are sure we have accurate and valid instances of application of the learning (something we have validated through our Success Case efforts), we can do simple calculations on the percentage and consistency of application. We can create a great discussion where people who have applied concepts share tips with people looking to apply that concept. We can even start to hone in on topics we could make part of our Community of Practice.

While a spreadsheet is good, I'm not sure it will have the emotional impact we are looking for in people who have not been in the room during the exploration. We decided to create the "Wall of Success." We will design a large, 4x6-foot graphic that has images of the children and families we serve overlaid with the key stages of the Center for Leadership journey. During the card sort exercise we will ask participants to write their accomplishments on premade 3x5 stick-able notes and place them on the

TABLE 9.1 Application of Leadership Concepts to Participants

Participants	Center for Leadership Concepts						
	Leading Change				Business Acumen		
	Integral Approach	Stakeholder Management	7-Step Process	Executive Communication	Assets	Interplay	NPV
Participant 1	O/N		O	N	O		O
Participant 2	N	O/N	O	O			O
Participant 3	O	O	O/N			O	
Participant 4	O	N	O	O			O/N
Participant 5			O	N	O		N

O-Areas where executive participants have successfully driven application
N-Areas where executive participants want to focus next

wall. When you step back and see all the accomplishments superimposed on images of the children and families we care for, it should be a very rewarding feeling for everyone. This will be great to share with our senior team during our graduation ceremony.

Thursday, October 12, 2006

I was driving home from our first-ever graduation event this evening feeling a great sense of pride. It was clear from the graduation speeches that the leadership development experience has made a tremendous impact on our participants. They each had a story of their journey: tales of trepidation and honor upon being selected for the program; evaporated worries about the time commitment involved; newfound relationships and perspectives on the organization and their role as a leader; renewed appreciation for their personal strengths and an increased confidence in their ability to lead; methods, tools, application, impact; physicians, clinicians, and administrators sharing a common bond and language of leadership—all these stories. Several people had taken on new roles and one person was soon going to be in conversation about a significant promotion. All attributed the Center for Leadership as a key contributor to these new developments. I'm proud of our participants for the way they dove in and made the experience their own. I'm proud of my team for tenaciously working through the hundreds of issues and sticking to the principles required to make this happen.

The presence of our senior team was especially important tonight. As they listened to the stories of personal change unfold and looked at the wall of success, you could see their understanding, pride, and support growing for these leaders and the Children's Center for Leadership. This was the emotional connection I was hoping for. Coupled with the quantitative evidence we collected, they will truly understand the full impact.

Just being there would have spoken volumes to our participants. Their words of encouragement and confidence in this
group of leaders touched everyone in a lasting way. Our senior
team has been invested in this journey and once again they have
demonstrated their commitment. Many times in organizations
different parts of HR are not aligned,
or in the worst case, mutually dis-
abling. This was not our case. Linda
and I worked as a seamless team to
diagnose issues and manage solutions. I'm proud of what we have created together, and it has reminded
me of the truth that it is not possible to make bold progress without committed partners and allies.

> Larry confirms yet again
> that winning the hearts and
> minds of managers is a vital
> pillar for success.

Tuesday, October 17, 2006

Thinking back over the past eighteen months it has been quite a
ride. Many times I was not sure how to get from point A to point
B. So many "how to" questions. Throughout the journey I always came back to a few simple things that guided me and kept
me energized. The first was a sense of conviction about why we
need to take on this challenge and that the results we need demand nothing less than the complex process we have adopted.
The easy and perhaps tempting way forward would have been to
take the promised resources and put on some "glow in the dark"
events—hotshot guru speakers, lush venues, dramatic agenda
items, etc.—that would earn rave reviews from everyone. We
took the road less traveled. We kept digging to connect to the
most pressing business needs and developed a truly HIL process.
As the program became real and natural resistance emerged, we
reminded ourselves and our senior team that the resistance is a
sign that we are doing something of significance that will lead
to true change.

The second is the understanding that even when the organization is ready, willing, and able to take on a worthy initiative, there are other initiatives potentially just as worthy. Many times people in the learning function feel that the senior-most leadership team "just doesn't get it." While this can be true, it is also true that business leaders need to make difficult choices about how best to use limited resources. The Finance Committee of our Board of Directors committed funding for the Center for Leadership over a multiyear time horizon. However, funds would be released each calendar year only after seeing evidence of impact. We welcomed the challenge to show our progress each year to the Senior Team, Finance Committee, and entire Board of Trustees. While it would have been nice to get all the monies up front, this approach puts leadership development on equal footing with every other major initiative designed to take the organization to the next level. I want our initiative to be judged as a business investment like anything else, not a special category immune from skepticism and inspection. Of course, the risk in this approach is that we would not have a compelling case to make and that the initiative would get derailed. But the pressure we imposed on ourselves to prove value helped us keep a continuing focus on creating impact.

> Larry again raises the bar for expectations and welcomes the challenge of being judged annually on the business value his program helps produce.

The third is transparency. I must have said the words "we're learning our way forward" a hundred times to myself since we started. It didn't mean that we released workshops that were half baked, or did not think through and implement all the surrounding processes required. What it did mean is that we consistently shared what was and was not working, and encouraged everyone involved to do the same. While we are an organization that, with good cause, strives for perfection in everything we do, the Center for Leadership is an initiative where not having to be "perfect" on day one was the only way to constructively tackle such a complex endeavor.

Finally, I realized at times that Linda and I had to hold on tightly to our aspirations for the organization. We always strove, through repeated communication, to make it clear that the leaders and therefore the program are owned by them not by the HR function. This was well understood and the majority of the time it was true. There were times, however, when Linda and I needed to stay firm in our resolve to keep going in the face of small setbacks and to remind ourselves of why we needed this so badly.

Thursday, November 30, 2006

"How did it go?" my wife asked when I got home from work today. "Pretty good," I said as I struggled to sum up the day's events. We presented our progress and future plans to our senior leadership team today. In the presentation we consolidated our Success Case work into a series of slides showing personal, operational, system leadership, and financial impacts. It was powerful to show the specific actions that brought these impacts to life. It was so gratifying for all of us to see and reflect on the results our intensive evaluation had revealed. When I write it all down, I'm amazed at how it really adds up.

In the area of personal leadership impact, we found:

- 360° feedback results across the class significantly improved.
- Most participants reported a strong message of increased confidence as a leader.
- Four people have received expanded or new roles.

- 100% of our participants have stayed with the organization and many have cited the Center for Leadership as a major factor in their reason to stay.

- All the participants said that the new relationships they made were priceless.

- All the participants said that they had increased their perspective from a very local or narrow view to a broader, more comprehensive view of our healthcare system and the industry in general.

In the area of system leadership impact, we found:

- The internal-to-external hiring ratio had moved from 40/60% to 57/43%.

- The language of leadership, methods, tools, and relationships were driving improved levels of leadership collaboration across the system.

- Center for Leadership leaders were achieving better retention rates in their organizations than in the overall system.

- We had reductions in our severance costs and expenditures on external consultants for projects our leaders were now equipped to handle on their own.

In the area of operational impact, we found that the application of Center for Leadership methods and tools had resulted in:

- New partnerships opening the door to new strategies and plans.

- Expanded current services and the accelerated ramp-up of new services.

- New partnerships were formed with physicians, who had reduced expenses in clinical settings.

- Improved delegation led to redesigned roles, the filling of critical positions, and the elimination of some planned personnel expansions.

- Improved processes resulted in enhanced cost control.

- Stronger leadership was demonstrated by the teams that report to the participants.

We found that when we added up the financial value of the personal leadership, system leadership, and operational impacts the class had achieved, the numbers were significant. The total value of cost savings and cost avoidance were in the multimillions of dollars as was the incremental revenue and external funding.

At the end of the meeting, we shared our recommendations for how we could improve the program and what we needed from senior leadership. We outlined our plans to significantly expand the program and discussed the financial support that would be required.

"Pretty good," I said. "We were approved for next year. Now we can really get started."

10

Case Example #2: The "So What?" Factor

Organizational Change at Clark County School District

DR. JEFF HAFEN
Director, Support Staff Training and Development

ost school districts are busy places. In a school district that has opened nine new schools every year for more than a decade, "busy" is an understatement. Such is the case in the Clark County School District (CCSD) in Las Vegas, Nevada, the fifth-largest district in the United States. The student population is fast surpassing 314,000. It employs more than 37,000 people, including 19,000 teachers, 11,000 support staff personnel, 1,300 administrators, 150 school police, and 6,000 substitute and temporary employees. The district has more than

337 schools within its boundary of approximately 8,000 square miles.

In such a vast organization, with its environment of rapid growth and all of the challenges that causes, why would any one employee attempt to initiate a new approach to conceptualizing and managing training? The training delivery burdens alone were staggering. An equally perplexing question is how does any one employee go about implementing a massive organizational culture change in terms of the way people are trained in an organization this large?

The answer to these two questions lies in the response to the "So what?" question. Some background information may be in order here to understand what I mean.

Since the early 1970s, I have been in the training business. In the late 1980s, I completed a Ph.D. in Education Administration with an emphasis in Business, Industry, and Government. As the director of CCSD's Support Staff Training and Development department, I oversee the design, development, implementation, and evaluation of multiple training courses and programs.

For quite some time I have been disenchanted with my training role, where the primary focus of my unit was to design and deliver training: in essence, providing skills and knowledge. My disenchantment was growing because I typically didn't have a clue what happened with the trainees after they left the training room and returned to their jobs. I called it the "So what?" factor. They came to training . . . we did a great job imparting knowledge . . . they learned some new things, but, "So what?" Seldom did I know what kind of impact the training was having on the trainee or the organization beyond the classroom.

I have come to understand that any trainer can do evaluations of their training based on Kirkpatrick's evaluation Level 1 (satisfaction/reaction) and Level 2 (acquisition of skill/knowledge). Sometimes Level 3 evaluations (application of learning back on the job) can be done. But in my experience, I had found very few organizations that had done a true Level 4 or 5 evaluation (improvement in performance or organizational measures)—especially with soft skills. For those few who had, the approach involved tremendous time and resources but did not produce very credible results that were useful. In fact, I made a site visit to one of America's largest corporate universities because they were touting how good their training evaluation process was. I arranged to take two or three days out of my hectic schedule, paid a substantial fee to be able to talk to the corporate training evaluators, and traveled to the Midwest so I could see what a Level 4 evaluation looked like. When I got there, after the opening session, I asked when I could see what they were doing for a Level 4 evaluation. Their response astounded me. They said that they were not really very good yet at Level 4 evaluations. I couldn't believe it! I felt like I had just had the classic "bait and switch" technique pulled on me.

From that point in the late 1990s, I truly felt like Level 4 evaluation was simply a theory—but nothing practical for much of the training being given in the district. There was this disquieting disconnect between what I felt I should be doing and what I was really doing. Don't get me wrong. I knew that my instructional designs were solid. I was confident that lesson plans and materials were high-quality. My training department enjoyed a reputation for delivering first-rate training seminars that people liked attending. Workshops were filled. And yet, I had this disturbing feeling that there needed to be more than just happy "butts in seats" measures. That is to say, what impact was the training having on employees after the training concluded? What organizational impact was happening because of the training endeavor? I knew the district was facing crushing demands for delivering thousands of hours of training to our new employees. That burden alone was formidable. But something in me looked beyond that to think about the consequences to the district, if that training did not really produce the results that were needed in terms of competent performance. What if we delivered all that training, but people in the new jobs couldn't really do what needed to be done? Where would we be then?

I was continuously on the lookout for ways training was being evaluated. It was truly serendipitous how I found out about the concept of High Impact Learning (HIL) and later the Success Case Evaluation Method process, which is now called the Advantage Way, a proprietary system of Advantage Performance Group (APG). One day late in November 2003, I was going through my incoming mail, sorting the important pieces from the avalanche of junk mail. I was struck by their announcement about training making an impact long after the training seminar concluded. Whoever designed that piece must have had people like me in mind. The announcement from APG was a small but extremely significant event. It gave me a glimmer of hope.

So, the first part of December 2003, the CCSD Operations Training Manager and I drove to Scottsdale, Arizona, with the hope of finding out something significant about Level 4 assessments. The session gave me an epiphany. All of a sudden, it became very clear to me how a Level 4 evaluation could be done, relatively simply and yielding useful results. My colleague and I were excited about the prospects of being able to measure what kind of impact our training might have once trainees got back on the job. Little did I know that the journey would take more than three years before the first HIL initiative and Success Case study would be completed.

One of the biggest benefits of the approach I learned is that people can be very definite about what their training dollars have bought them. Personally, great satisfaction has come to me because I can now answer the "So what?" question. It is hard for us obsessive/compulsive folks to be in training. When working with people, especially in the soft skills arena, it's easy to know where you are beginning but hard to know when something is finished. I think that's why I like to vacuum. I know where I started and where I ended. I can see the sweeper lines in the carpet. The Advantage Way helps me to better assess the "sweeper lines" in training.

Even though I now knew what needed to be done, I still had to figure out the "how." I had to confront multiple challenges as I forged ahead implementing the process. Although money is always a barrier in public education, budget was not our biggest challenge. The principal hindrance wasn't even getting people to buy into the idea. The biggest impediment was getting people to actually do business differently—to move from accepting the concept to making practical application of the concept. This was especially true for getting managers to do things differently to actively support training, since this was a true culture change.

It has been my observation that managers' behavior related to training tends to fit into these five categories: preventing, discouraging, neutral, encouraging, or requiring. Unwittingly, managers can be a hindrance and hurdle rather than a help to employees who are learning new skills, knowledge, and attitudes (SKAs). Sometimes trainees return from our seminars excited about the newly gained SKAs. Then they are clubbed with the "Yes, but . . ." bat. For instance, after the trainee animatedly explains a new and exciting concept gleaned from a training seminar, a manager, supervisor, or co-worker says, "Yes, but . . . that will never work here." There are multiple variations on that clubbing theme, such as, "Yes, but you really don't think that applies here, do you?" or "Yes, but I prefer we stick to our tried and proven way of . . . ." These kinds of responses can quickly prevent, discourage, or neutralize the use of new learning. One of the new precepts we took to heart completely is that in order for training to be used on the job and have a lasting effect, trainers need to partner with supervisors/managers who agree to actively participate in the training process with their direct reports. Trainees need supervisors/managers who encourage and even require application of the newly gained SKAs.

So, here I am in a district of 37,000 employees and the only one with the knowledge of the Advantage Way HIL process and Success Case approaches. I felt like the Lone Ranger. But I knew I had to do something to overcome inertia. Talk is cheap, so I thought I'd show the CCSD world the tremendous benefits of using the HIL process and Success Case procedure. If I could demonstrate with a real project the results this approach could get, I might win over enough followers to keep the ball rolling. In my first attempt to conduct a training project in the Advantage Way environment, I searched for a project where the supervisors would be amenable to using the process. I knew I could not make this work alone, and I especially needed a champion in a leadership role.

> Jeff decides to be a pioneer and begins the process of bringing allies to the cause.

During my efforts to find a project where we could implement the methodology, my esteemed colleague Karyn Wright got exposed to the Advantage Way. She was sold on the concept and committed to help push the idea along. Karyn is the director of new teacher training for the district. In addition to her focus on training for licensed personnel (e.g., teachers and project facilitators), she is a huge proponent of training for support staff employees as well as other employee groups. I couldn't ask for a more skillful and good-hearted comrade in arms.

Karyn was gearing up for the upcoming New Teacher Induction training that begins in August each year, just prior to the opening of a new school year. Approximately 1,500 to 2,000 new teachers need to be trained each year. This is training of a huge magnitude. There could be a temptation to rush and finish. However, even in light of the enormity of the task, Karyn is not willing to do just "good enough." She realizes that the training has tremendous implications on the core mission of the district.

And she was also frustrated with not knowing whether the specific training she and her staff were delivering was really "sticking" after new teachers left the training seminars. She knew how badly she needed the training to work, but was not at all sure that it really would. I asked her how principals and other line administrators were following up on what new teachers were being taught in New Teacher Induction seminars and if they encouraged teachers to use the new skills. Karyn indicated that she could not answer that question with a high degree of confidence. She knew she did not have a way to measure if lessons learned in the training were being applied back on the job in the classroom. There needed to be certainty that there was a connection between what went on in training and what goes on in the classroom. Karyn was determined to share with other colleagues the impact that the Advantage Way process could have on her program and other programs.

Through my discussions with Karyn, it became obvious to me that I needed to modify my original game plan from rolling out just one initial successful HIL and Success Case project. I needed to get multiple people involved in rolling out several training initiatives concurrently using the Advantage Way process, if we were going to get any traction.

Karyn and I began promoting the Advantage Way with key training personnel in the district. Steadily, more and more of them became eager to engage in the process. As a result, in February 2006, Karyn and four of her direct reports as well as twelve other district employees became certified in the Advantage Way.

We were now in a situation where multiple Advantage Way projects could be rolled out all at once. First lesson learned: two people promoting an idea (as opposed to a solitary voice) can have an exponential impact on the organization in selling a new concept.

The February 2006 Advantage Way certification seminar was a huge success in many ways. We had licensed employees, administrative employees, and support staff employees. These participants came from Support Staff Training and Development, Operations, Enterprise Resource Planning (ERP), Technology, New Teacher training, Administrative Leadership, Food Service, and the East Region Superintendency—seventeen people total.

Each group had one or more projects they brought to the certification workshop. They all got good starts on planning their projects during the seminar. A particularly rewarding outcome was that the East Region superintendent, assistant superintendents, and administrative assistant espoused the HIL concept and began promoting it wholeheartedly in their area. Within a short time, their region alone was conducting four or five training initiatives in the context of the Advantage Way process.

> Jeff raises the expectations for training results with a senior leader in the organization.

Additionally, the word was beginning to spread that if people wanted to create a unified, measurable Line of Sight and tie training to business results, the Advantage Way was *the* way to go. I received requests to hold another certification seminar.

Strategically, we had made a big splash. It was wonderful to have so many people espousing the Advantage Way concept. Tactically, I felt secure that having more people onboard would yield a greater number of training initiatives that would be conducted in an HIL environment.

Despite the growing number of certified staff members from a cross-section of the organization, it was still hard to turn the concept into practice. As you might suspect, it was difficult to get managers and supervisors to take the time to learn about the seminars they were sending their direct reports to. Even more difficult was getting them to commit to sit down with their direct reports and conduct an Impact Map dialogue. (See Chapter Three for more information on Impact Maps.) I'm not sure why they didn't feel comfortable sitting down with their folks to help set the stage for skills acquisition. I guess they just didn't understand the WIIFM (what's in it for me), and thus were unwilling to make the time in their busy schedules for a process that they were not sure would pay off.

So, we then started a two-pronged approach for initiating Advantage Way projects. First, we initiated several projects using the process. These projects were ones that originated in our department, such as the Support Staff Leadership Academy, Customer Services, and so forth. The second approach was to find a sponsor who was willing to endorse training done in the context of an Advantage Way environment. The second approach, finding a senior sponsor, has paid by far the greatest dividends. For example, the East Region sponsored a Diversity training initiative for about 100 people. The Transportation department sponsored a train-the-trainer workshop. Student Data Services sponsored a working styles seminar. There were others as well, including the Clerical Academy, which Support Staff Personnel sponsored.

> Despite resistance Jeff is tenacious in finding partners in the organization who are committed to getting results by following the process.

In each case we told the sponsoring department that we would host the training (arrange for the facilitators, materials, and training space), deliver it, and evaluate it if they would promote the pre-event activities, such as co-authoring an Impact Map, and guarantee that their people would participate in an Impact Booster session. Additionally, department heads needed to give their consent that their employees could participate in such post-training event activities as a web-based training evaluation/survey and an over-the-phone interview. Second lesson learned: Find someone with a "pet" training project that they are totally invested in and hitch your wagon to it. And by the way, make it as easy as possible for them to focus on the rollout/follow-up process.

Here is a case in point. Earlier I mentioned the Clerical Academy training initiative, which has been one of our most successful offerings to date. The reason this training was so important to me is that it was not only tactically critical, but also strategically crucial. The purpose of the training course was to help prepare principal secretaries new to the position to be highly competent as soon as they entered the position.

The Clerical Academy focused on preservice training for elementary school clerks who were aspiring to be promoted into the position of elementary school office manager. The office manager position is critical at a school because the person in that position serves as the administrative assistant to the principal in addition to directly or indirectly supervising multiple support staff employees. The office manager sets the customer service tone for school sites. This person is called on to make critical decisions regarding schedules, people, and ideas. In the absence of an administrator, the office manager informally takes the key management role at a school. She or he is like the oil that tries to minimize engine friction at a school site. Needless to say, one of the most important hiring decisions a principal makes is who will be the office manager.

With anywhere from 2,000 to 4,000 people each month moving into our community, the number of school children is swelling. Therefore, for the past decade, on average we opened a new school every month of the school year in our district. Because of this, there are a lot of openings for the office manager position. Historically, keeping a well-qualified pool of office manager applicants has been a huge challenge for the district.

In the early fall of 2006, the Support Staff Personnel department in the Human Resources (HR) Division partnered with my department, Support Staff Training and Development department, to begin putting together a preservice training component for the elementary school office manager position. It was critical for HR to recruit people who could fill the office manager vacancies. It basically was a "grow your own" initiative. The Support Staff Training and Development department designed, in collaboration with Support Staff Personnel, an academy specifically for elementary school clerks who wanted to become elementary school office managers.

> Jeff partners with the key stakeholders in the district and raises the expectations for how training should be implemented and the results it can achieve.

We set several things in place to ensure the success of this critical development program. One contributing factor to the huge success of this program was that prospective participants had to agree to finish all thirteen learning modules before they could receive credit for taking the course. Equally important, the participants' supervisors also had to sign a letter of commitment stating that they would support their direct reports in completing each learning module and sign off on any out-of-class assignments. This approach paid off handsomely!

Here's how it worked. When participants were screened and cleared to attend the first Clerical Academy, they and their administrators were notified. At the same time, participants and administrators were informed that the first of the thirteen modules (having an Impact Map dialogue) was to be conducted by the participant's administrator. This was a gutsy move on our part to get the administrator involved in the learning process. We believed firmly that development is a whole-organization responsibility, but we didn't know how they would take to being held accountable for conducting the first module with their trainee.

Nevertheless, participating administrators were sent the Clerical Academy Impact Map. They were given instructions on how to conduct an Impact Map dialogue and a due date for conducting it. To their credit, they then reviewed it with their direct reports. Our department made phone calls to the administrators to confirm that the dialogues between the administrators and the Clerical Academy trainees had been completed before the beginning of the second module.

At the beginning of the second module, the facilitator asked for a show of hands of those whose administrators completed the first module (Impact Map) with them. Every hand was raised. This was like a payday for us! It was our first training initiative in which all participants had participated in an Impact Map dialogue with their supervisor. And what's more, it was evident throughout the course that they all understood what was to occur and why. What a success! Administrators, facilitators, and learners all had the same Line of Sight. Each one understood how the successful completion of the Clerical Academy would contribute to the business results that would lead to the achievement of district goals.

Other elements helped make this program successful. It was set up right. The HR department identified a critical need and established eligibility criteria for participation. Administrators and supervisors were onboard before the training classes ever started. Participants understood both the organizational and personal benefits that would be derived from successfully completing the training. There has been a desire on the part of the administrators and participants for work skills to be practiced on the job during and after the training classes were completed. It is the best example of all stakeholders involved having an intentional, tactical, and clear Line of Sight.

In fact, the positive reputation of the Clerical Academy is such that office manager candidates who have completed the Clerical Academy seem to be better prepared and more competitive for the open positions. To date, it has been one of our most successful joint training ventures. It has been highly visible, tremendously helpful to key administrators, superbly supportive for secretaries, and totally results oriented in helping accomplish business processes. Banking has benefited, payroll has been processed properly, customers have been cared for, and other critical actions have been accomplished so that schools support student achievement.

The data compiled during the Success Case Evaluation Method process were revealing. One participant was able to complete payroll accurately and on time *the first time*. She also provided evidence of other results derived from the Clerical Academy, including an increase in teamwork, positive customer service and public relations, as well as more positive staff relationships. She stated that there was a dramatically improved front office climate and efficiency.

Another course participant relayed: "By working with my office manager following each class, we both have a better understanding of the needs of others. I am able to be a backup for her and she is able to rely on me to help her."

I'll share one final comment made by one of the trainees: "Before I went to the Clerical Academy classes, I knew nothing about budgeting. After the training I was able to go to the web site and see what balances and encumbrances we have. I am also able to locate, complete, and submit personnel requisitions.

After the class, I was able to practice that task, but just today, I was able to 'do it' for real and I did it right."

Question: What is it worth for an organization to have its support staff know and be able to execute critical tasks required for the smooth operation of a school the very first time, like correctly using customer service skills, appropriately carrying out the budget process, and properly employing the hiring process? A lot!

For me personally, the strategic component of the Clerical Academy was as important as the tactical success. Specifically, now that HR had a global understanding of the Advantage Way process and Success Case Evaluation Method, it was at least three times faster to get the next preservice training initiatives implemented. The training rollout matrix, if you will, was in place. Three other preservice clerical academies for other job positions have begun for the 2007–2008 school year. The strategy of making the Advantage Way an integral part of our training culture is starting to happen.

As we partner with more departments and regions in the district, we anticipate more and more tactical and strategic successes. It is now a matter of constancy and perseverance.

As I look toward the future, one of our biggest pushes needs to be in marketing ourselves and our successes. Our story needs to get out. The more well known we become within CCSD for linking supervisory personnel and training participants to business results, the more people will allow us to help them increase the return on their training investment. I love the idea of becoming a training results investment broker.

ISO 9000* has helped us to get our story out. Our department became ISO certified during the process of our incorporating the

---

*ISO 9000 is a family of standards for quality management systems maintained by the International Organization for Standardization (known as ISO).

Advantage Way into our district. Part
of becoming ISO certified is demonstrating that training is effective.
What better way to do that than by
using the high impact learning process and Success Case Method Evaluation? In fact, our ISO consulting
team was so sold on the concept that they now are telling other
prospective ISO certification candidates to see us about the
Advantage Way in order to fulfill the training component of
the ISO certification process.

> Jeff's department has made great progress in raising the expectations on how training should be implemented in CCSD.

Because of the public trust that school districts have, I would
love to see other districts around the country incorporate the
Advantage Way into their organizations. It is so helpful when a
public entity can show the positive impact their funding dollars
are having. Legislators, grant administrators, and taxpaying cit-
izens can all look upon education with a higher degree of confidence when they know money is being spent responsibly.

To sum up my experience, let me share an insight with you.
Many years ago, I learned about the concept of sine qua non.
This is a Latin phrase meaning an essential condition or element; an indispensable thing. Literally it means "without which
not." I suppose in the modern popular vernacular it could translate to "*the* hot button."

I remember a story told about the modern sewing machine.
For centuries, the eye of the needle was at the top of sewing ma-
chines. One of the reasons the modern sewing machine could
exist is that a very creative person saw that the eye of the needle
needed to be at the point of the needle. That one breakthrough
coupled with an oscillating shuttle gave rise to the modern
sewing machine. The sine qua non for the advent of the sewing
machine was the eye-pointed needle along with the oscillating
shuttle. Those things revolutionized the sewing industry.

My personal feeling is that the sine qua non for training in the Clark County School District, and maybe training in general, is the Advantage Way—the HIL process coupled with the Success Case Evaluation Method. For me, it has been *the* hot button, the critical ingredient. When we successfully push the Advantage Way button, we know that competency and skills combine to generate critical actions that produce key results leading to the achievement of goals. This is the essence of what training is all about.

I started out asking a rhetorical question: In such a vast organization with its environment of rapid growth and all of the challenges that causes, why would a training leader attempt to initiate a new, pervasive, and bold approach to conceptualizing and managing training? The answer is that I believe so strongly that Advantage Way has been for us the sine qua non triggering a transformation in how we do business. It clearly has answered the "So what?" question.

11

Case Example #3: Raising Expectations for Concrete Results

Leadership Development at Holcim

LISA BELL
Manager, North American Learning Center, Holcim

ome people love a parade. I love a challenge. Although, I can't say that I dove in head first when the opportunity came across my desk to launch a Learning Center for the North American companies of Holcim Ltd. I'm not a corporate daredevil by any means. I prefer to take calculated risks. I had to be sure this was the right next step for me and for the company.

Within Holcim North America, there are two independent companies operating side by side: Holcim (US) Inc. and

St. Lawrence Cement Inc. in Canada. Both companies are leading suppliers of cement and related mineral components in their respective countries. Holcim (US) operates seventeen manufacturing plants and more than seventy distribution facilities, while St. Lawrence Cement is even larger and operates 100 different facilities in Canada. Together, the companies represent $2.5 billion in annual sales. The North American Learning Center (NALC) would be responsible for creating a learning culture across an enterprise of two separate companies serving almost 6,000 employees.

Patrick Dolberg, President and CEO at Holcim (US) and Philippe Arto, President and CEO at St. Lawrence Cement, posted the position for a director of the NALC in the summer of 2005. Both companies had historically made significant investments in training and learning, yet the CEOs recognized that in order for Holcim North America to be the best in our industry, we needed to do even more to develop our people, and we had to be sure that learning investments drove the business results we needed to stay competitive. They felt that a NALC could help identify strategic learning priorities that directly impact the performance of both companies (enterprisewide) and roll out comprehensive training programs that produce sustained results.

At this time, I had developed and was managing the central Staffing and Development Group at Holcim (US). Prior to that role, I had started the company's university relations program. My background also includes procurement, account management in consulting and special events, as well as company relations work at the University of Michigan's Ross School of Business.

Though I did not have much experience with corporate learning, I was all too aware that when companies couldn't determine the impact of training, they tended not to see much value in it. If I was going to spearhead the initiative, I didn't want to be in the situation of chasing return on investment (ROI). I wanted to be ahead of the game versus having to justify value and budgets.

.Through my research and networking I ran across the High Impact Learning (HIL) Systems approach developed by Rob Brinkerhoff. From this approach and from my networking it became crystal clear to me that the key to sustained results from training was to tie the learning to the issues that matter most to the business and to get managers involved. Measuring training's impact on the business makes a learning culture a culture of accountability. I began to realize that even with great intentions and top-rate tools, the NALC wouldn't add real value to the company without a way to inspire managers to execute the changes on the job. It would be the managers who would have to help employees make the link between what's learned in training and what they are supposed to do with it once they get back on the job. I began to formulate a vision of what a learning culture would mean to the company. I saw learning as an enterprisewide process, not just a series of isolated events. I could picture the collaboration between Human Resources (HR) and people in the field responsible for training—managers and employees—working to apply learning on the job and celebrating the results when business objectives are met or exceeded. I knew this was the right challenge to accept, and I knew I could help build something new and meaningful for Holcim (US) and St. Lawrence Cement. I took the job—and the challenge.

I was quite certain about where I was heading and where I wanted to end up, but far less certain about what specific steps to take to get me there. I knew too that, given the newness of the learning center and my newness in taking on its leadership, everyone would be watching. It struck me that my first foray into offering learning services had better be good. I wanted—and needed—to start with a "win."

When I met with each of the CEOs individually, the same thing was stated in both discussions: Patrick and Philippe both wanted a learning culture and they wanted training to work—that is, to change behavior in ways that impact business daily. They knew that despite the strong commitment to development and training present in the two companies, we had not done enough in some areas. In many cases, either the training we had done didn't stick or it was a "flavor of the month" with little follow-up or follow-through. Both CEOs expressed a strong commitment to staying the course with a new learning strategy and seeing sustainable results. I already believed that the HIL process is what we needed to use to shape our learning culture. Hearing from both CEOs individually that they wanted a learning culture and sustainable training results—I knew we were on the right track.

My goal then was to leverage HIL with our first initiative to get a quick win and begin to change the culture. But I knew also that I could not just score a win in one small area of only one of the companies. The initiative I opened with had to be important enough to draw support, linked to business results that mattered, and importantly, had to span both the Canadian and U.S. companies. Achieving my first initiative goal and effectively launching the department required me to complete three primary objectives. First, I needed to include as many key people as possible and ensure that my intentions were transparent, clearly working in the best interest of both companies. Up to this point, most people in the company viewed training as an event. Second, I wanted to get people to think of training as a process that involves managers. My third objective was to convince the organization that when people try to apply training to everything, it

> Lisa begins to seed the message that business impact is a whole-organization accountability.

ends up being applied to nothing; but when it's applied to a specific objective with success, it then has the best chance of getting applied more broadly. In my earliest discussions with senior leaders, there was a clear focus on less-tangible skills, such as "better leadership" and "more effective people management." I had quite a challenge getting people to understand that "soft skills training" could indeed be used to impact a measurable business result. I began my campaign by hosting an HIL workshop for thirty-five people with training responsibilities or involvement (HR managers, technical trainers, line managers with interest, etc.). These individuals came from across both companies. They would be my grassroots champions, so their buy-in was crucial. Fortunately, the workshop was extremely well received, and they were excited to implement the process in their areas.

> Her bulldog quest for relevant business results leads her to successively focus on increasingly more specific outcomes.

At the strategic level, we established two key stakeholder groups in November 2005. The Work Group was made up of a subset of those who participated in the HIL workshop, and the other team was a Business Advisory Group. This group consisted of senior managers in the business. This formulation gave me a critical mass of learning and HR staff who understood our conceptual approach, and a group of hard-nosed business leaders who would set our business direction and (I hoped) send a message of accountability. The Work Group was the team that would develop and recommend the North American learning strategy, structure, and focus areas that would be presented for approval by the Business Advisory Group.

> Lisa raises the bar, locking in expectations for concrete performance and business outcomes.

We called our first project "Foundations" because it was about determining the foundation for the learning strategy and the focus of the NALC. Ultimately, we had to meet the needs that the CEOs requested of us. To make this happen, I knew that our key stakeholders had to buy in to our strategic direction and have a chance to shape our understanding of the key business challenges. With the help of Advantage Performance Group (APG), we interviewed forty influential business leaders from across both companies and began to draft Impact Maps that reflected our understanding of the critical performance and business issues. We interviewed all members of the Business Advisory Group and twenty-five more key stakeholders in the business. When we set up the interviews, these individuals expected that we would be asking about their views on training and learning needs. Our strategy was to come at these interviews from an unexpected direction and surprise them a bit by our focus on the business. In the actual interviews, we spent twenty to thirty minutes asking about business challenges. The interviews served many purposes. First and foremost, we had to get information about our companies' key business challenges as well as those in each person's specific area. We used the time to explain to these top leaders the NALC's focus on business results. Lastly, the interviews allowed these individuals to have a say, to understand what we were doing, and to be champions—all because they were asked in the right way.

> Lisa begins to plant the perception that learning staff are business partners, not event-delivery people looking for suggestions about what training to offer.

As the Business Advisory Group and the Work Group were forming, I knew it was imperative for the teams to hear directly from the CEOs regarding their expectations for what the NALC would be focused on and do. This would be a powerful and memorable way to create the common vision and raise every-one's expectations for training to the same high level. So, I arranged for both gentlemen to be on the phone together at each group's first meeting. This was how I could ensure that we started right out of the gate working in alignment with

> The expectations bar gets set higher.

executive expectations. At the Work Group's first meeting, we interviewed Patrick and Philippe in the same way we did the other key business leaders, asking them:

- As you look out the next twelve to thirty-six months, what do you see as the top two or three key business challenges for St. Lawrence Cement, Holcim (US), or across both businesses?

- What is your greatest fear about the people of St. Lawrence Cement and Holcim (US) not being able to deliver against these goals or challenges?

In addition to discussing the business challenges, the CEOs expressed their desire to see us generate the beginning of a strategic framework.

Allowing the group to hear firsthand from the CEOs was a strategy that worked well to raise expectations for the NALC and the two Holcim organizations. The forum also gave Patrick and Philippe the opportunity to listen to each other's answers. Together, we saw our alignment or lack of alignment. Most importantly, we had the chance to demonstrate our focus on business results to the CEOs. From that point forward, after every key learning strategy development milestone, I set up a call to provide an update of the groups' work to the CEOs. I wanted them to see progress, provide feedback to shape the direction, and make sure we were on track with their expectations. I felt it was also good for Patrick and Philippe to know our steps along the way. After five months of the groups working together toward our goals—while I was continuously selling everyone on the importance of applying training to a specific business objective—I had won a Holcim (US) sponsor and gotten the green light to test HIL in three business units in the United States and Canada. It is fair to say that at this point we had effectively raised the level of expectations within the organizations on the business impact that training could have. The somewhat scary realization sank in at this point that now we had to live up to those expectations!

Managers and supervisors in the three business units would participate in a program we had titled "Building Leader Performance," which focused on improving coaching and performance management skills. The intention was to support the Executive Committees' strategic focus on developing leaders and building these leaders' capabilities in two areas: driving accountability and execution. The Real Learning Company's *Symphony* and *Conductor* workshops were the training platform we chose for addressing the gaps in coaching and performance management skills. We built the HIL process around them to help drive accountability and execution and to ensure that the coaching skills would get applied in important job tasks. We would use Impact Map discussions between managers and participants both before and after the workshops to set expectations and ensure a strong link to specific business objectives.

Our sponsor, a Senior Vice President for the Southeast Region, selected a facility in South Carolina to be the inaugural demonstration project. We helped leaders in that facility create an overall Impact Map that linked the training to their measurable targets for safety and housekeeping, the business results that they agreed were most vital to address. These were issues that affected many areas of the organization, including manufacturing, logistics, and sales. The second demonstration project was at a St. Lawrence Cement facility in Canada that linked the training to a very different business objective: improvement in overall equipment efficiency. The third demonstration project was for another St. Lawrence Cement business unit with yet another business need; this group wanted the training to be clearly linked to an ongoing effort to reduce net working capital. So we weren't just doing leadership development and hoping that participants figured out how to apply the skills on the job. Instead, we were targeting critical issues in the business and setting the expectation that managers would lead the charge for these critical initiatives.

> Lisa climbs way out on the expectations limb; while the workshop on performance management skills is the same in all three businesses, the business leaders and participants see it as three very different training initiatives, each focused on business goals unique to their needs.

Having training so clearly and tightly focused on concrete and measurable business outcomes was a significant paradigm shift in the two independent companies that challenged us to win the hearts and minds of two executive teams, two multilevel management teams, and two legions of employees. I knew from the start that getting both companies onboard wasn't going to be easy. Because I had the two CEOs' support, I hadn't anticipated that it would be that difficult to get people onboard with the changes. Over time, I came to understand that the communication and leadership effort would be essential to the success of this first initiative. I also came to realize that this would be trying, frustrating, and oftentimes draining.

As with any initiative of this scope and complexity, nothing goes completely smoothly. This effort was no exception. One of the recurring obstacles that we faced was getting all of our business leaders and managers to change their mind-sets. Even though we had communicated many messages about the HIL concepts and the focus on business results, they were accustomed to making quick decisions about training and then moving forward to roll it out pretty much as a "one size fits all" and getting as many people through as fast as possible. As tempting as it would have been to go with the flow, I knew that in the long run delivering training that wasn't connected to the specific business goals of the facilities would not lead to measurable value for the organization or a lasting culture change.

To make sure there were mechanisms in place to tie the training to the targeted business objectives for each facility, Building Leader Performance incorporated a daylong Impact Booster for managers of trainees to fully engage them. The notion of managers attending the Impact Boosters and then conducting Impact Map discussions with their employees was foreign to our organization. There was considerable resistance to what was perceived as "extra steps" in doing the training at several turns, but I recognized the Impact Boosters as essential steps for creating accountability and alignment. I was tenacious about the importance of these steps and had to relentlessly repeat the message throughout the implementation. There were temptations, I admit, to offer a shorter version of the Impact Booster, but since managers themselves had asked to experience at least a part of the training, I held fast to the one-day format. If some did not participate as a result, so be it—I would have my control group for comparing results after the workshop.

In the Impact Booster session, we spent the morning helping the managers understand the HIL process. We emphasized their critical role in making training stick. In the afternoon, we gave the managers a taste of the *Symphony* and *Conductor* training. In this way they could understand and support what their direct reports, the facility supervisors, would learn and apply from the full *Symphony* and *Conductor* workshops. Two weeks after the Impact Booster, supervisors at the facility participated in the *Symphony* workshop. Thirty days later, they completed the *Conductor* workshop. By spreading out the training workshops, we were giving time for managers and supervisors to have their pre- and post-training discussions and to practice the new skills.

As it turned out, the Impact Booster sessions, meetings between managers and supervisors before and after the workshops, and the training itself worked together very well to motivate learners to apply the training to the performance areas they needed to improve. The Success Case Evaluation report for the South Carolina facility told a story of resounding success! We were able to demonstrate that the training led to measurable results for the business in its critical need for improving safety—results well beyond what one would normally expect from this sort of training had it not been augmented with the HIL procedures. We had taken the HIL concepts and made them work for our operations in the United States.

I realized early on that getting the message out and raising the standards in people's minds for what we can achieve and how we need to go about implementing the training process was critical for changing mind-sets and building alignment and support. It is like a political campaign in which the candidate is trying to rally the populace by painting the picture of the possibilities and raising expectations in the

> Lisa is relentless in getting the HIL message out, again and again.

minds of the constituents by keeping the message front and center. We continuously looked for strategic opportunities to build partnerships and alignment with the executives throughout the company. One such opportunity to educate them and gain their commitment occurred in May 2006. We convinced the whole

Executive Committee of Holcim (US) to preview, and even experience parts of Building Leader Performance and the HIL process. This was key to gaining their full buy-in and support for the program and its three key elements: (1) the training modules, (2) aiming the training at a business result that matters for each executive's area, and (3) engaging managers and learners in accountability for performance results through HIL.

Another great opportunity we orchestrated was having all thirty-five officers of the company experience *Symphony* and HIL at the December officers' meeting. Once they experienced it for themselves, I knew they would understand and be hooked. Having them participate firsthand was much easier than trying to explain it in words. My boss and I agreed that the best way to get on the agenda was to have the suggestion come not from HR, but from one of the other two Business Advisory Group Members on the Executive Committee in Holcim (US). I spoke directly with the sponsor of the South Carolina project and with another Business Advisory Group member who was highly involved. They liked the idea and proposed it to the whole Executive Committee at their next monthly meeting. The idea was accepted.

Armed with coaching from members of the Business Advisory Group and the positive results from the Success Case Evaluation report for the Carolina Plant Market System that was hot off the press, this strategic workshop at the officers' meeting was a success and helped us advance our cause. We were able to show the Executive Committee the business results (i.e., improvements in safety and housekeeping metrics) that the training was helping to drive, as well as connecting the actions of managers (i.e., following the HIL process and having Impact Map discussions with employees before they attended training) with the results.

STICKING TO THE CAUSE
AT ST. LAWRENCE CEMENT

Although we were making progress in Holcim (US), the demonstration projects at the St. Lawrence Cement facilities had more bumps in the road. There had been three significant personnel changes in senior management, which caused a slight delay in order to reengage stakeholders and solidify project sponsors.

The head of HR and a regional Senior Vice President, both of whom were members of the Business Advisory Group, left the company. It was taking longer to find sponsors for the Building Leader Performance demonstration projects without the executive sponsorship on the Business Advisory Group on the St. Lawrence Cement side. Because the CEO at St. Lawrence Cement was eager to have all the managers and supervisors speaking the same language about performance management and coaching, it would have been easy to just rush ahead and roll out the *Symphony* and *Conductor* training across the company with just a "taste" of the HIL approach included.

> Lisa accepts a delay in implementation, despite resistance, to be sure the business goals and HIL process are truly owned and bought into by senior leaders.

I knew, though, that this would not help in the long run. I kept remembering my early discussions with the CEOs, in which they communicated that they wanted a learning culture and that they wanted training and results to be sustainable. They didn't really know what it would take to do this when they uttered those words, and neither did I at the time. However, this was a "moment of truth" in which we had to stick to the cause and not take the easy path just to be able to show progress or succumb to short-term political pressures. If we just did the training, we would completely miss the opportunity to demonstrate the difference and the results—and we would miss the opportunity to start to change the learning culture. Certainly, it isn't a onetime shot, it would only be the start—but without the right start we would give up the opportunity completely.

I presented the concepts and explained the benefits to the company in several meetings, but too often the decision makers were not present. I finally "sold" the sponsor of the two demonstration projects in Ontario by sending him information and then asking to talk about it over a group dinner at a senior leadership meeting we were attending. Maybe it was the food and drinks that did the trick, but I think it was more the persistence and passion of my discussion. (OK, maybe it was my desperation!) He could probably tell he wasn't going to be able to brush me off easily. At the dinner, he asked one of his direct reports to meet with us afterward. At this quick meeting, his direct report became one of the project sponsors in Ontario. With each instance of turnover, I had to start telling the story over again and building the case from square one. In some ways, I'm sure it might have been politically less risky not to try to push the issue of bringing Building Leader Performance coupled with the HIL approach to St. Lawrence Cement. But I just never considered it, because I knew this was the right way to shape our learning culture and ultimately to bring sustained results from training. Believing in the process and remembering the early discussions I had had with the CEOs, I never questioned staying the course.

RESULTS

Each Building Leader Performance project focused on improvements in a key business objective selected by senior management of the three business areas in Holcim (US) and St. Lawrence

Cement. The stories reported in the final Success Case Evaluation illustrate specific areas where the training played a critical role in helping to achieve the results. From better management of networking capital in one facility, to efficiency improvements in another, to safety and housekeeping improvements in a third, there are numerous documented cases of how the Building Leader Performance training provided significant cost savings and operational effectiveness for Holcim (US) and St. Lawrence Cement.

In December 2006, we presented the results to the Holcim (US) officers. They were impressed by the fact that 90% of participants had applied some aspect of the training on the job—a result that, in fact, surprised even those of us in the NALC. But our verification of these instances of application of learning confirmed our success: 44% had applied what they had learned and had already gotten results, while the remainder had taken clear action to apply the training but had not yet documented business results. The contribution of the managers' involvement was strongly verified: 75% of the people who achieved measurable results had Impact Map discussions with their managers, whereas the trainees with lower impact experienced significantly fewer instances of manager involvement and support.

Our leaders at all levels were impressed that we measured the results and measured them in this way. The interviews revealed that people were seeing changes in behavior relative to the business objectives (no accidents, better and more frequent safety and housekeeping observations, and timely closure of related issues identified in the observations). The Vice Presidents were enthusiastic about the results and gave us their support to continue rolling out the program—in the same "focus on specific business results" way—in other facilities.

The St. Lawrence Cement facilities also had solid results and the Success Case Evaluation reports for both facilities provided clear proof that the HIL process was much more effective than stand-alone training. One facility's data revealed that 67% of the participants applied what they learned and nearly two-thirds of those got tangible results. In the other facility, 64% of participants applied what they had learned with more than 40% of those achieving tangible results. Beyond the solid business results, we found that participants who followed the HIL process (e.g., defined in this case as those who met with their managers before and after training) applied what they learned twice as frequently and were three to four times more likely to produce measurable results than those who did not. As the three demonstration projects were our first round of HIL programs, we were realistic about the fact that the quality of the discussions overall was probably not that high. But still, the results showed that it made a huge difference to have the discussion and complete the Impact Maps. I can imagine the significant results we will see when we get even better and more disciplined about having these discussions before and after training. Still, these early findings gave us the conviction to press forward and work diligently with leadership in the other locations and to hold their managers accountable for using the HIL process.

LESSONS LEARNED

Along this journey I have gained many valuable insights. I realized that while I need to be tenacious in establishing the framework and focusing on the business outcomes, at the same time, I need to be patient and adaptive with my partners in the business. For instance, I had to integrate Building Leader Performance in a way that made sense at St. Lawrence Cement, which was not necessarily the way it was done at Holcim (US). It has taken me awhile, but I've resolved myself to the fact that each new stakeholder is going to have to go through their own personal learning curve at their own pace. I know now that starting with the basics, I'm going to have to step each emerging leader through the concepts and earn their trust and support in order for us to achieve a

> Lisa confirms that she had to negotiate tactics but stood firm on the principles that guided her work.

learning culture. Perhaps one of the most gratifying and confirming instances of the progress we have made is the fact that, at the time of this writing, line managers involved on the HIL process have stepped forward and requested that *more* time be devoted to the Impact Boosters. Initially, one of our biggest concerns was that managers would never give up their precious time to participate in the "extra" steps we asked of them. And now, lo and behold, they themselves have asked for more. Will wonders never cease!

My conviction and the clarity of the NALC's vision keep me going. It all makes so much sense and is really very simple. Yet it is not always easy to communicate. And people and organizations don't turn on a dime. Over the past couple of years, I've had some defining moments where I've wanted to bail out but it's not in my nature. I took on the challenge of building the NALC from the ground up because I like to watch departments come together. I'm motivated by the finished product. I know there are peaks and valleys in the journey, but the patience to stay the course has been such a huge reward. The talented team of people who make up the NALC carry the message of training as a means for impacting business results across all areas of both companies. Our collective passion is driving change in the organization. The new mind-set is starting to live and grow on its own merits not just because of our persistence.

The Success Case Evaluation reports played a key role in our success in winning over hard-to-convince leaders. The results from the demonstration projects have given us the credibility

we need with executives, supervisors, and employees to influence changes in various areas of the company. For example, in
May 2007, the executive sponsor for
one of the Canadian Building Leader
Performance demonstration projects
sent out a bulletin announcing a
process improvement project as part
of our Enterprise Resource Planning
(ERP) software system in which they
would partner with the NALC and
follow the HIL process. He did this on his own without any
prompting from us, because he saw the value in the new process for turning training into business results. It was a solid win
to have strong backing communicated from the field.

> Lisa lets the data do the talking, telling the story of how efforts from across the entire organization made the results possible.

My advice to anyone embarking upon or in the middle of an
Advantage Way initiative is to make sure you are committed to,
and have extreme clarity around, your vision. You have to know
exactly what you are trying to achieve. Reach out to industry ex-
perts and other business leaders who have done what you are
attempting to do. Use this mastermind group to test and validate your strategy. Once you have solidified your vision and
strategy, find the simplest way to express it. Whatever you do,
don't vary your pitch. I've learned through trial and error that
constant and *consistent* communication is the key to successfully implementing cultural and process changes.

When you are launching the process, be armed with talking
points at all times. Like me, if you are passionate about leveraging learning for measurable results, you are going to want to tell
the whole story from beginning to end. However, most people,
especially executives, do not want chapter and verse. People
want to hear from you what they need to know in the simplest
of terms in order to make sound decisions. Focus on the business results and do not be afraid to raise their expectations

about what is possible. The catch is, you have to be brief and you can't make people connect the dots for themselves. After all of the creative ways I came up with to describe HIL, I found "learning as a process" to be the most understandable for people new to the concept. Once you have your talking points down, be prepared to repeat your message again and again. You are not boring your audience. You are helping them learn. (Remember, repetition is the mother of learning.)

Also get ready for opposition. If you're not meeting resistance, you're probably not working on something that really needs to be changed. Don't expect people to eagerly catch your enthusiasm for change. Chances are you are an early adopter of innovative ideas. Recognize that most people, however, need more time than you to shift gears and see the value in new ways of doing business. And my final words of advice: have the courage to take the risk.

12

Case Example #4: From Training Delivery to Trusted Advisor

Sales Force Transformation at Insight Enterprises

JULIE DERVIN
Vice President of Learning and Development

oday, August 2007, Insight Enterprises (Insight) is striving to be an information technologies (IT) solutions provider that partners with our clients to enhance their business performance through innovative technology solutions. We have strong partnerships with clients in enterprise, small to medium business, and public sector markets. Currently, Insight has more than 4,500 employees worldwide and serves clients in more than 170 countries. When I started with Insight in April of 2000, our strategy was based on a transactional sales model, differentiating from competitors on the basis of low cost and high availability. As the industry landscape began to change dramatically due to the dot.com bust and other market factors, it became more and more evident that Insight's value proposition of being the low-cost, high-availability provider was no longer a viable differentiator in the marketplace, but a mere requirement to remain competitive in our industry. The company's senior leadership recognized the need for Insight to transform into a total IT solutions provider in order to create a different type and a higher level of value to our customers.

Like many organizations trying to make a shift to "solutions," initially we did not realize the magnitude of what it would take to move from a transactional-based selling environment to a more sophisticated solutions provider. This posed huge challenges for the organization in its quest for transformation, especially in the cultural, behavioral, skills, and knowledge arenas. It was a very challenging time for me as a leader who had responsibilities for the "people" aspects of the business. I knew how critical addressing the "human side" of the business was if we were going to be successful, but our business leaders seemed to see it differently and focused more on the operations and systems. From my and my team's view at that time, we thought we were doing the right things by proposing performance management programs, various leadership training solutions, and change management interventions along the way to support this transformation. For other reasons, however, the business leaders at that time chose not to support these recommendations. In fairness, I realized I was not looking through the same big-picture lens as were the senior level leaders who were making decisions on where they needed to invest and the trade-offs that had to occur in the business. So for a period of time

I trusted that there were logical reasons behind the decisions and actions they were taking, even if none of these was addressing the people side of change, skills development, or employee engagement.

By the mid-2004 time frame, my awareness of the philosophical differences I had with my company relating to the human side of the business had reached its peak. As a director having responsibility for supporting employee engagement and learning and development programs, I realized my department was considered more of a *benefit* than a function that was instrumental to supporting the organization's success. As I reflected on all the proposed but never fully implemented training strategies; all the employee development programs that had potential to have so much more impact than they actually did; all the one-off, unaligned training events we were commissioned to run that were supposed to "fix" something—it was evident where our place was in the business. That was always a hard pill for us to swallow because we felt we could be adding so much more value, and my team and I knew our employees were so hungry for this support.

> Julie realizes that she and her training function are caught up in a decreasing impact and influence cycle, and that it is time to do something about it.

Although we kept trying to deliver the best training and development solutions we had resources to provide, we could never get enough traction with our solutions to demonstrate quantifiable impact in order to get the attention of the business. Like the Greek mythological character Sisyphus, we felt like we were always pushing a huge boulder up the hill just to watch the darn thing roll back down again and again and again. We've all been there at some point in our careers. While I was proud of the fact that in certain pockets and isolated areas of the business my learning and development team produced some high-quality, cutting-edge programs on a shoestring budget, I knew in the grand scheme it did not matter because these things were not valued by the business.

As challenging as it was for me and my team to know we could be adding so much more value, the sales training group seemed to be experiencing even greater issues and more frustration than we were feeling. At that time, the sales training group reported into operations as a distinct and separate function from my department, which reported into Human Resources (HR). The sales training group was attempting to support a sales force that was experiencing some real challenges around attrition, continuous and incremental change, and leadership turnover.

Then in August of 2004, *it* happened. I remember the meeting vividly. My Senior Vice President of HR said to me in our regular update meeting, "Now, don't flip out, I did not commit to anything, but there is something I want to explore with you." And the words came out, "What would you think if we moved the sales training function under you?" The sales training group was reporting into a newly appointed sales operations executive who approached my boss admitting he had no idea what to do with them, because he had no experience in training and development. He asked my boss if this function could be moved into my department and if I would take on the responsibility. Knowing all the challenges that would come with that assignment and the fact that the organization up to that point had never invested in any significant amount of professional selling skills for our sales reps, I calmly asked, "Why do they believe moving the sales training function to me will solve anything?" I knew the issues were not solely training related and moving that function to me would not get at the root of the various problems that existed. After further discussion with my boss, we finished the one-on-one with the agreement that I would at least think about it. My first instinct was to run as fast and far as possible.

But, I didn't and I am glad I didn't. The risk I took has been well worth it.

In hindsight, the timing of this proposal was perfect. It occurred to me this new challenge could be an opportunity to demonstrate the value of training and development in the more quantifiable environment of sales. Even though I knew I ultimately was not in a position to actually decline the proposal (from a career perspective), I saw it as chance to "put a stake in the ground" and discuss upfront what I needed from the business if this sales training group was going to be successful under my direction. So I proceeded to write a list of conditions under which I would accept responsibility for the sales training function. The theme of the list was to ensure the sales executive leadership had "skin in the game" and that there were expectations for concrete contributions to results calibrated and based on their level of investment (or lack of). I reviewed my conditions with my Senior Vice President and then with the Senior Vice President of Sales Operations and a few of the other critical stakeholders. To my delight (and surprise), they all were in agreement and seemed supportive. So naturally to avoid any future states of "collective amnesia," I did what any self-respecting (and slightly paranoid) director in my position would do. I drafted a follow-up E-mail with all the agreed-upon points, sent it to the appropriate senior executives, and filed all of their replies in my CYA folder. I mention this as an indication of how little respect I believed the learning and development (L&D) function received from other parts of the organization at that point in time. But this was all about to change in a very positive way.

In the following weeks we navigated through the changes of realigning the sales training group under my department. The

> Julie sees an opportunity to make a stand.

two areas I had to get my arms around were new hire sales training and a formal sales skills development program. One of the commitments I had with the senior-level leadership was that Insight would make a significant investment in partnering with an outside training and consulting group that had proven expertise in transforming and upgrading sales skills of an existing sales force from transactional to value-based selling. So my first step was to launch a request for proposal (RFP) process to identify an outside partner. While I may have had in my mind an ideal partner, I knew that if L&D chose the vendor exclusively it could be a reason down the line for anyone of them to "opt out" and do their own thing. The outlook remained promising as everyone we needed to participate seemed invested and even excited.

Then, in November 2004, a small miracle did happen. Insight announced its new CEO, Rich Fennessey, who came to us from IBM. Our new CEO came onboard and from the start made it known that employee development was a priority. He did a quick survey of the landscape and could easily see the people challenges that existed. He immediately supported our effort to completely overhaul the new hire sales experience and was extremely eager to invest in sales skills development for the current population of reps. My guess is that, as the new CEO, he knew he needed an early win that would begin setting the tone for his tenure. The timing was perfect with the RFP process just getting under way. While I am sure he wondered why we were going through such an extensive process to select a vendor, he played along. To my surprise, he rolled up his sleeves and jumped right in to actively champion the process. That was the point at which I knew this was really going to happen! By February of 2005, the contract was awarded to Advantage Performance Group (APG). The approach we were looking for and what they proposed was a very holistic and comprehensive strategy that was designed to ignite and support the behavior change required of the sales force to drive Insight's new vision of becoming the *trusted advisor* to our clients.

While the background work was under way for planning the sales training curriculum, which we named Insight World Class (IWC), our CEO and some of the other Sales Executives decided in the short term to move forward with an additional incremental sales skills training program from another training company. At the time, I was of the opinion that this short-term training event would be a wasted investment for the company and the approach (what seemed like "cattle herding" of 600 reps through sixteen hours of lecture-style sales training) was contrary to what we were trying to do with IWC. I raised red flags with my boss and explained why I thought this stopgap training would not be very effective. But in our discussions, we realized that the executive staff had to do something right away for the sales force and that even though it might do little to help drive the new strategy, it probably could not hurt. We made a decision to not stand in the way and save our battles for the more strategic and vital IWC initiative.

In June of 2005 my team and I were certified in the Advantage Way framework and Success Case Evaluation Method—processes we would use to ensure the results of our learning investment and measure its impact. I knew that IWC could not be implemented the same as any other training initiative we had done in the past; the stakes involved were high as we were promising measurable business outcomes, the amount of the investment was very large, and the initiative had a high profile and visibility. I recognized that this was my opportunity to really do training the right way.

As part of the certification process, my team had to complete a full Success Case study, so we chose to assess the sales training event that just occurred as the training program on which to conduct our first study. We finalized the evaluation in October

2005 and then reviewed the findings with the President and the Vice President of Sales. The study validated what we suspected from the beginning about the stopgap training: the only real impact that sales training event had on the business was a temporary morale boost. It was comforting to have solid data in hand as I was carrying this message to the President and Vice President of Sales. It gave me the confidence to tell it to them straight because the conclusions were irrefutable.

The President acknowledged the findings and stated it was OK because "we" needed this morale boost—albeit temporary. And looking back, he was so right. The environmental conditions at that time were not conducive to learning new skills and behaviors; the sales organization needed that gesture to begin trusting leadership again and to understand the new direction and focus of the company first. However, our CEO next commented on the rollout for the IWC sales training, emphasizing the need to make sure we get more than a morale boost this next time around. Then he opened the discussion up for recommendations. The synergy between the meeting discussion and the contents of the Success Case study could not have been scripted better. The Success Case study substantiated that sales managers were not coaching and reinforcing the learning back on the job, the reps did not understand how to assimilate the new skills into their sales process, and there was no system of accountability in place for either group to follow through on these actions. The data enabled me to engage in a very concrete and objective business discussion for shaping the IWC work going forward, doing it differently, setting the standard for what would be expected of the sales managers and reps. It felt like a very different type of discussion than ones that I had had with

> The door opens for Julie and her staff to promise more strategic and concrete results.

executives in the past, which had been more focused on delivery logistics and content explanations.

I recommended the Impact Map as a tool to use for the IWC sales training that was coming up in a few months. I proceeded to explain how it is used before, during, and after training; the roles of the manager, participant, and leadership; and the value of applying this more systematic framework. Since the President and the Vice President

> Julie uses the Impact Map to win buy-in for broader accountability.

of Sales were still fairly new to Insight and the current culture, I also explained where I would need their support if we were truly going to make this work, and I reminded them by referring to our overall Impact Map of the business results this initiative was intending to help achieve. I was delighted that they both were fully committed to my request. I recall leaving the meeting feeling different, like our work was respected and valued and that we had just entered into a real partnership with the business where all parties had skin in the game.

As we approached Phase 1 of the IWC sales training in January 2006, we began a communication process that was designed to consistently cascade the message and strategy within all levels of sales management using the Impact Map as the communication vehicle. My team worked with our President to shape the content for the Impact Map, and we trained sales management on what it was and how to use it. The Impact Map was the principal vehicle for ensuring that all levels in the sales

> She is relentless in communicating the business case and expected results for the training.

organization—from the executives down to each individual sales rep—held similar expectations and an understanding of how their role fit into the sales strategy. So there was no ambiguity around expectations, our President addressed the sales management group on how he wanted the maps used for pre- and post-training coaching discussions with each sales rep.

To further ensure the training participants' focus, our President recorded a video that was played for the sales reps at the beginning of each initial IWC Phase 1 session. Having an executive sponsor on video to kick off a training session is not totally unique, but there was a subtle but important difference between what we did and what is typically done in this type of video. In this video he covered exactly the same points covered in an Impact Map pretraining discussion:

> The raised expectations that Julie drove now pay off in getting high-level support for managerial accountability.

why they were attending the training, what new skills they were expected to learn, how they were expected to apply them back on the job, and how all of this aligned with the business results and organizational goals

These pretraining activities sent a very powerful message to all sales management and reps about how critical this investment was to the future success of our company. All of the pretraining activity and focus was very new to the Insight sales force. It created a very strong sense of priority and importance around training's role in the organization by enabling them to clearly see how the learning, if applied back on the job, would support the organization's goals of becoming a trusted advisor to our clients. It was an amazing new experience for me and my team to see how something so seemingly simple could have such a powerful effect. Because we were able to establish the linkage between the training and the business goals, we were much more successful in gaining management support and leveraging this to ensure that the successful execution of the training initiative was an organizational priority. That was my first experience of having a training initiative that was accomplished through a true partnership with the business where our leaders and managers participated and took accountability for their role in the learning process.

By March of 2006, we had completed the IWC Phase 1 training of all sales reps and were very excited about our newfound partnership with the business. Energized by this success, we could not wait to start the Success Case study to see what the difference in business impact was from this new approach compared with the previous training event. As we conducted the evaluation study, it became apparent to me that real organizational behavioral change was not as easy as one simple injection of a new tool. I realized it was going to take persistence, discipline, and continuous baby steps of improvement over time on all of our parts.

The study brought forward the issue that all sales managers were still not consistently engaging in post-training coaching discussions with their reps. Managerial involvement and support, as was identified in the first Success Case study, was still a problem. This finding prompted us to propose a different path for Phase 2 of IWC. We realized that going forward with the second phase, rolling out more training to the sales reps without the vital managerial support in place, would drastically under-

> The IWC initiative hits a pothole, but Julie sticks to the principles with an unpopular decision.

mine impact. We proposed to the President and the Vice President of Sales that instead of running the reps through the next five additional modules of training that were originally planned, we would use some of the Phase 2 training budget to design a coaching strategy for the Vice President of Sales and his management team and run the reps through only two new training modules. This was a difficult concept to get the sales management team to buy into. They first reacted by expressing concern that if they went with a coaching strategy and less actual sales training, they were somehow getting less for their investment. Running all 600 sales reps through five more training modules felt like a more tangible investment because a "butts in seats" metric was a more straight-forward calculation than a management coaching strategy. I could not blame them for originally reacting that way because sometimes that metric is still most comfortable for us training professionals too.

> Like a good business goal bulldog, Julie reminds the leadership that this initiative is all about the results, not the training.

At that point in the discussion, I leveraged the case study findings to reinforce that we still had the same problem that was identified in our very first case study and continuing to just do more sales training was not going to get at the root of the problem or get us closer to the desired sales goals and outcomes. We explained that the new proposal was cost neutral, not costing them any more or less, but just redirecting the resources toward what the Success Case data was telling us would yield a higher return at this point. After processing the information a little more, both key executives agreed to go with our proposal. For myself, as a leader looking out for the best interest of the company's assets, it felt really good to know I was adding value by providing advice rooted in facts on where Insight would be better off investing its money.

> Julie has to flex her backbone to say "no" when a key senior leader's commitment waivers.

In preparing for the IWC rollout of Phase 1 for the other two sales sectors, I was working directly with the Vice Presidents of those sales sectors. I encountered one Vice President who held the old Insight mind-set that saw training as a *nice to have* and not really a critical part of the strategy. Several attempts at trying to get him involved in the design work and building the content for his division's Impact Map failed. It dawned on me that if we were having this much difficulty trying to gain involvement and cooperation during the design process of the Impact Map, this obviously was not a priority for him. In the past, I would have just urged my team through their frustrations to keep moving forward the best we could, working around his lack of engagement. However, now that I knew I had the President's support to approach the training as a true business improvement process, and after reflecting on the expectations for results that we had built, I felt emboldened and duty-bound to address this issue head on with the Vice President. Because I had the business goals clearly in my mind and the data from the previous Success Case studies in hand, I was able to approach this as a *business investment* issue and not as a *training* issue. I knew I was going to see him at an offsite meeting in the next week so my plan was to have a discussion during a break. We met briefly and I let him know my team and I had been trying to schedule some conference calls needed to complete one of the tools we use for the training implementation. He responded very apologetically, stating they were so busy managing the sales numbers, he really did not have time for this other activity. In a very, nonemotional tone I replied, "So in the grand scheme of things this doesn't seem to be a priority right now." I went on to say, "That's OK if that is the case, you're not going to hurt any feelings here. Our goal is to support you in reaching your goals, and if this training is not a priority right now in helping you do so, let's discuss putting this on hold." To even further put him at ease and remove any potential feelings of conflict, I told him that postponing the training for his sales sector would not be a bad thing for my team either, as we were so

Julie negotiates tactics, but does not cave in on principles.

stretched trying to support the other two sectors. He gingerly proceeded to admit that, in fact, this was not a priority and thought putting the work on hold was a good idea. So the Vice President and I went to the President and let him know about the decision we had made together to not move forward with IWC training for this sales sector for now. Our President supported the decision, as he was not about to invest in training if the most senior leader of that sales organization did not see it as a priority due to other pressures at that time.

It was the most liberating feeling to go back to my team to let them know they could stop "banging their heads against the wall" with this part of the project and begin focusing on the other two sales sectors that were ready for the training. My team was a little disappointed to bring the work they had already started to a screeching halt, but I explained how we have to stop wanting for the business what they do not yet want for themselves. This was a new era for our training department; we were no longer pushing that proverbial boulder up the hill. We now had leadership in the business that valued employee development and had serious expectations for results, and that's how and where we were aligning our work and resources from then on.

Another example of where the organization and managers lost their focus during the rollout occurred in July of 2006, when we launched the IWC Phase 2 modules for the initial sales sector. The first two sessions of the training were completed and my team noticed that reps were not very engaged and that managers in the sessions were not participating and supporting the facilitator. I was also getting feedback from the Vice President of that sales sector that these sessions were not going as well as

Phase 1. Further, the facilitator leading the sessions stated that when he asked the class whose manager reviewed the Impact Map with them only a few hands went up. The "red flags" immediately went up in my mind as I considered this information. I knew something was very wrong. My training manager who was responsible for the workshop sessions called a huddle with our APG partner and the Vice President to recalibrate. They proceeded to have a very candid conversation regarding what was going on and each left the meeting taking accountability for their pieces. The Vice President agreed to get with his managers and set clear expectations for their role in the training sessions. Our APG partner took the action to get with the facilitator to tighten some of the exercises and to review the Impact Maps with the participants at the very beginning of each session to identify any reps who might not have had the pretraining discussion with their manager before coming to the training. Because of the partnership and involvement by this Vice President, we were able to

> Julie gets a reminder that business impact is a whole-organization accountability.

quickly get a training session that was going sideways back on track. In reflecting on what went wrong that caused this rocky start into Phase 2, we realized we had made assumptions that the sales management would naturally pick up their roles where we left off in Phase 1. As with any organizational change, the new behaviors and processes don't happen overnight. It takes time for everyone to be doing those things routinely as second nature. We reaffirmed that it was going to take persistence, discipline, and rigor over a longer period of time before we could expect the business players to naturally assume their new role and responsibility in the training and development process at Insight.

LESSONS LEARNED

Today, in August of 2007, I look back over the past three years and see where we are as a L&D partner to our business. I have experienced both sides of the coin: working with leadership that did not regard employee development as a strategic lever and then working with leadership that valued it as a critical investment to drive the execution of a company's strategy. My experience has taught me several valuable lessons. First, that active executive involvement is the single most important ingredient in managing a training function that strives to deliver true business impact. Second, having a systematic process and tools to engage managers and other key nontraining personnel and also to measure the extent to which all our actions together drove business results were crucial. Without these methods and tools, I would have had the desire to promise results but could not really have delivered them. Finally, having the process and the data gave me the personal strength of conviction so I felt comfortable taking some risks, asking for commitments on the part of senior management, and trying out some new approaches. What I have found quite interesting is that we know that the largest percentage of learning takes place on the job, but yet we still find our leadership and internal clients wanting to recast the corporate training professionals as the sole "owner" of employee development. My perspective has changed dramatically over the past three years in understanding our place in the business as a provider of services, tools, and programs that support management in *their* responsibility for developing the skills of their employees. I have thoroughly enjoyed and appreciated the sponsorship we have with our new leadership and have all the confidence we will reach our vision of being the trusted advisor to our clients (if we haven't already). My staff who have been through this journey with me joke that it feels like we've worked for two completely different companies without ever having switched jobs. We agree that we like our role in this *new* company much better. The days of grassroots efforts and trying to drive training and development initiatives from the middle have finally been put to rest for my team, and we continue to look forward to each new challenge our leadership brings us.

13

Getting Started on the Courageous Training Path

A few years ago one of us was touring the Mayan ruins at Chichen Itza in Mexico. The largest pyramid there—Kukulkan—seems to grow out of the ground and soars above the jungle a remarkable 25 meters high (80 feet), about the height of an eight-story building. It is a common practice for tourists to climb to the top of the pyramid. There are 365 steps (one for each day of the year), each step very narrow in depth, but considerably higher in rise than the typical staircase. In addition to the architectural and engineering phenomena, one observes another more human phenomenon that occurs daily at the pyramids. People tend to climb the pyramids—all 25 meters of them—facing the rock, using all fours, as a child might go up a set of stairs for security. For many people, once they get to the top above the treetops and turn around and gaze out over the jungle, their fear of heights—perhaps even if they did not previously know it—kicks in with a jolt and they realize getting back down safely is a serious problem.

With your back pressed firmly against the rear wall at the top of the monument you look down what seem no longer to be steps but something more like a staggeringly steep and stepless slide. Crazy thoughts race through your mind: Are you stuck up here for the rest of your life? Is there a helicopter service that brings you back? Why did you ever climb up here in the first place? You are frozen in place. Finally you calm your irrational thoughts and get focused on the reality that you must indeed climb down. You figure out a workable strategy and with the encouragement of friends or strangers, you begin a descent. The method is embarrassing, but works. You sit twisted on one side of your bum, you twist your body and neck as best you can so you are looking at the reassuring rock wall behind you and not the vast open space underneath you, and you lift and lower your body one step at a time. After a while—there are many, many steps—your confidence grows and you are even able to look outward and "enjoy" the view.

We disclose this tale of personal frailty because it resonates with the advice we give to a question that is always tossed our way. Having delivered hundreds of presentations on the concepts and methods we write about in this book, we can always count on one question being asked: "So, how do you get started?" Our advice is similar to the travails on the pyramid. You don't implement the Courageous Training process in the same fashion in which most people scramble up the pyramid: quickly, without a plan and a devil-may-care-attitude. Instead you start the journey more like the trip down the pyramid. The trip begins with the recognition that staying where you are is no longer an acceptable option and that you want to get to a better place.

The Courageous Training leaders with whom we have worked have begun their journey with this emotional commitment first. They have recognized that they are truly not satisfied with the current state of affairs in their professional training and development world and that they want to work differently and accomplish something better than what they have known in the past. At some point they admit to themselves that "good enough" is not good enough; that the way training is being done now is not working well enough. This dissatisfaction and their desire to make more of a difference are strong enough that they make the decision to get started in a new direction. They summon up their courage and commit to getting started even though the first few steps bring anxiety and unknown but certain risk.

After this act of will, they are ready to consider the rational steps they should take to get started. While everyone's road map will differ in detail, we can distill some useful guidelines and suggestions that are garnered from our experience with the dozens of bold leaders in our user group.

START SMALL—DON'T TRY TO CHANGE EVERYTHING ALL AT ONCE

Rome was not built in a day and the hole into which training has descended has been dug deep over several decades. You cannot leap out of the hole all at once. We have seen two major variations on the "start small" theme, one of which has worked and one of which has not.

Some professionals with whom we have shared our approach at professional conferences and workshops have latched onto one or two of the methods or tools, such as mandating Impact

Maps for every single training program offered by their organization. Despite their good intentions of trying to use one or two of the tools or concepts across the board to lift business impact, they mostly find that their efforts were too diluted. They ended up with little or no improved results to show for their trouble. Starting small by trying to do just a few pieces of the overall process everywhere, we have found, usually gets you nowhere.

The second approach is to do all of the process in only one place. This approach is far more likely to get results. It is far better to systematically implement the process and tools for a single project and make it work than to nibble around the edges on many projects or initiatives. So, for example, the most progress has been made by those who have worked carefully to select a single initiative, such as these illustrations below:

- A sales training effort that will be deployed with just one sales force as a part of a larger new product launch
- A performance management training program intended to boost safety metrics in a single production plant
- A new leadership development program being tried out in one division of the company
- A training initiative sponsored by a vice president in a business division who has specific goals he or she wants to accomplish

All of these examples are alike in that they are more contained efforts within a smaller organizational unit. They are alike also in that each has a single or more limited sponsor or "champion" (discussed in more detail below). The tools and methods that support all of the Four Pillars are knitted together into a systematic whole. *It is the whole process together that brings results, not the single application of any of its pieces.*

AIM FOR EARLY WINS

Starting small does not mean picking a safe little training project hidden away in the shadows that no one cares about—one that no one will notice if it succeeds or fails. Starting small means picking a project that can become a showcase and making it work. Courageous leaders have learned that another best practice is to find an initiative—one that fits the parameters of the previous recommendation—that is still relatively high profile, that really needs to work, and that someone in senior management does not want to see fail. Selecting this type of project puts training leaders in a high-leverage position where they can still exert practical control but at the same time they cannot turn back—going part way down the pyramid steps gets you nowhere. They have to make this initiative work, for themselves, for their internal customer, and for the organization. Then they implement the Courageous Training process in a comprehensive way, ensuring that the right resources are in place throughout all parts of the implementation. Courageous Training leaders play for the important, "the showcase," win without spreading themselves too thin across multiple efforts all at once. They know an early win will give them a compelling story about the business results that training was able to help produce for the organization when they need to enlist the support of the next senior manager about a High Impact Learning (HIL) project.

WORK WITH A CHAMPION

This recommendation is really a corollary of the first two. Courageous Training leaders know the importance of executive "air cover" (described in Chapter Five), so they look for senior leader champions who meet the following selection criteria:

- They are in charge of an initiative about which they care—
  one that they wish to succeed, that is important in the
  larger strategic scheme of things, and that has a reasonable
  chance for success (i.e., is not a doomed effort to begin
  with).

- They know that training is a key component in the possible success of the initiative.

- They are concerned that "training as usual" will not be
  good enough to ensure their success and are willing to try
  out a new approach.

- They are people with whom the training leader can work
  compatibly.

The training leader works with the senior executive champion to help implement the initiative and makes a commitment to the success of the effort. In short, the training leader volunteers his or her services to do whatever it takes to make sure that the training achieves the results needed by the executive sponsor. In return for this all-out commitment, the training leader asks the executive sponsor to commit to holding direct reports accountable (as the training process prescribes) for the support actions that are necessary to achieve the business goals that the two of them—the training leader and the champion sponsor—have mutually agreed to.

Many colleagues in our user group have followed this approach with success. They have looked for and found a senior champion sponsor who appreciates people development, with whom they have worked successfully in the past, whom they anticipate would be receptive to the concepts of the Courageous Training approach, and with whom there is a track record and a degree of trust. In short, the first project needs to be around an important issue and in the camp of a senior executive with whom the Courageous Training leader can work to manage the project so that it can be successful.

BUILD A CADRE OF ALLIES AND SUPPORTERS, USE A TEAM APPROACH, DON'T TRY TO DO THIS ALONE

Courageous Training leaders recognize early on that they can't be the Lone Ranger in making the first project successful or when beginning to implement new approaches to any training. They build a cadre of allies and supporters that will help them work their way along their journey. (After all, even the Lone Ranger had Tonto to help him out of some tight spots.) These allies sometimes are colleagues in their own department, they may be in line management, or they may be trusted advisors from outside the organization. The most successful Courageous Training leaders are skillful at developing all varieties of allies because they recognize that sometimes they need a guide in the process who has been there before; sometimes they need advice on the politics and hot buttons of the internal client; and sometimes they just need a like-minded training colleague who can be a sounding board for them. Readers will find allusions to this principle in all of the four case example chapters. All of the members in our user group have expressed a similar notion, noting that they needed the support of allies, and to some extent they have all looked to other members of the user group to provide some of this external resource.

One cannot make the Courageous Training transition strictly as a solo effort—and the corollary to this guideline is that there must be some level of senior leadership readiness for and interest in a new direction. One could not make this approach succeed in a totally negative culture or leadership environment.

Notice that in each of the case examples there was at least a faction within the senior leadership ranks that needed results and looked to training to make an effective contribution. This senior leadership faction does not need to know exactly what it needs or precisely how a new approach will work, in fact they probably never will. But they do need to have a belief in the value of Human Resources (HR) and a notion that training can make a worthwhile contribution.

TELL THE STORY, TOUT YOUR RESULTS FAR AND WIDE

We have mentioned several times in this book that Courageous Training leaders do not seek self-serving credit for themselves or their department for the successes that are achieved. By the same token, it is counterproductive to keep the results hidden. Just as their job is to show the organization when and why training *doesn't* work, it is also their job to inform and educate the organization when and why training *has* worked. They need to help all current and future stakeholders of training see the connection between the process, their behaviors, and the results. The message must be truthful and it should focus on the positive results and learnings. The options for ways to share this information are many: publish the story in company newsletters, conduct end-of-project meetings with senior stakeholders, and produce formal reports and present them at executive meetings. Courageous Training leaders recognize that changing how their organizations do the business of training is a change process and, as with any change process, the organization needs continuous reminders of successes to keep it energized and interested in continuing.

BE PREPARED TO MANAGE THE TRANSITION AS A CHANGE PROCESS

Courageous Training leaders know that starting off with the correct mind-set is essential if they are going to achieve long-lasting results. They recognize that implementing the Courageous Training approach is not a quick fix proposition, but rather a change initiative designed to alter how their organizations fundamentally approach the business of training. Like all journeys, this one starts with the first step—beginning with that first project that produces the win for the organization and the Courageous Training leader—and continues with many more down the road.

Courageous Training leaders set a long horizon and are prepared to see the change through. They are realistic about what they can achieve and how long it will take. They can promise increased business impact in a relatively short time frame—a matter of months—on a project-by-project basis, but they also make it clear that the concept and practices of the whole-organization process for training success is a multiyear effort. Recognizing that the road is long does not cause them to satisfice and nibble around the edges; they still look for the high-profile project that can get them an early and big win. But they recognize that after the first tactical challenges of making it work once, there is the larger strategic challenge of driving the approach into the "DNA" of the organization so that it becomes standard operating procedure for how training gets done.

Courageous Training leaders know that, as with any change process, they can expect some resistance along the way and are prepared to handle it. As one member of the user group has said, "If you're not getting any push back when you try to implement the process, that means one of two things. Either you have died and gone to heaven or you're not working on the right things." When working on the important projects and trying to get managers to make some fundamental changes in how they do things, there will always be some conflict or resistance. Savvy training leaders are prepared for these potholes in the road.

LEARN AS YOU GO

As Larry Mohl pointed out in his case example (Chapter Nine), a "learn your way forward" strategy is the hallmark of a successful change management effort. Training leaders cannot suggest that they have all the answers and proceed as if the process were a cookbook with rigidly prescribed steps for the entire journey. Instead they set the expectation that the best way forward cannot be fully known beforehand and will emerge over time through an iterative cycle of planning, doing, checking, and planning again. They approach the leadership task humbly but with confidence that the way forward is possible and vitally important, and that feedback and reflection will sustain them all.

STICK TO THE CODE!

Our last bit of advice: heed and stick with the Courageous Training Code presented in Chapter Seven. It springs from experiences, observations, and reflections we have discussed together over the past five years. We have yet to meet a training professional among the thousands we have encountered in our many workshops, seminars, discussion groups, and presentations who does not *agree* with the principles in this book. Everyone believes it makes sense and is the right direction.

What has differentiated the truly successful colleagues

we know from the many thousands who simply agree with the principles is that they found the courage and personal conviction—the belief that there was no turning back and only one outcome was good enough—to take the *action* to bring the Four Pillars to life. Although they didn't have the code written in their personal handbook when they started their journey, they were unknowingly living these principles to bring about important results and changes for their organizations and for themselves personally. The code we proffer comes from them through reflection and revisiting with them about their experiences. Our best advice in closing is to follow this code and stick with it. It works.

Resources: Terms and Tools

All of the authors who wrote case examples for this book refer to a common set of methods and tools known as the Advantage Way system. This system was created by Advantage Performance Group (APG) and is APG's proprietary version of High Impact Learning (HIL) Systems, a conceptual framework, methods, and tools developed initially by Robert O. Brinkerhoff (see Brinkerhoff and Apking 2001). The system helps training leaders design and implement learning interventions that are certain to help training achieve increased business impact.

The purpose of this Appendix is to help readers understand the components and terms contained in the Advantage Way system. The core principles of the Advantage Way are explained in Chapter Four: that is, effective training is a process that begins well before and continues well after the training event is delivered. The Advantage Way process and the many tools contained in each step of the process are shown in Figure A.1.

Over the past four years, and especially since the inception of the user group, many variants have been developed for each step in the process. Thus, the process is not a lockstep prescription, but a framework used to augment and guide a training implementation. The Advantage Way methods and tools are embedded into the implementation of a training initiative, thereby creating the alignment, clear expectations, accountability, and metrics to significantly increase and measure the business impact of that initiative. These tools are available to certified members of the Advantage Way user group.

Figure A.1 The Advantage Way Process

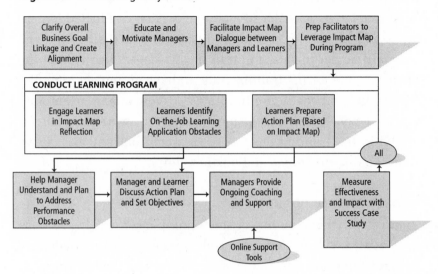

THE ADVANTAGE WAY GLOSSARY

To help readers understand and interpret elements of the case examples that may not be immediately clear, we have provided the glossary of some of the less readily identified parts of the process shown in Figure A.1.

Creating Focus and Alignment with Impact Maps

Impact Maps were explained and illustrated in Chapter Three. They are used to depict the business linkage of a proposed or existing training initiative. They are created by the Courageous Training leader in conjunction with training clients and sponsors at the initiation of the training process. They reappear again in Impact Booster sessions to help managers understand the business case for training; they are used in manager/trainee dialogues before and after training, during the training program itself, and yet again as part of the results measurement process.

Impact Booster

An Impact Booster is the educational session conducted to help managers prepare for and support those among their employees who will be participating in training. Managers learn about the business case for the training, how to have an Impact Map dialogue with trainees before training, and how to engage employees in a post-training dialogue to support an action plan for applying the training on-the-job in ways that will best drive individual performance and business impact.

Impact Map Dialogues

These are brief one-on-one or small-group meetings (face-to-face or virtual) between managers and trainees in which managers help employees create a Line of Sight between the learning outcomes for the training and their intended on-the-job performance that will contribute to business goals, and for which their managers will hold them accountable.

Obstacles Survey

This is a web-supported or paper-based survey in which trainees forecast the probable performance obstacles they believe they will face when they try to apply new learning on the job. The obstacle survey results are reported to managers along with a guide for the mangers to use when helping their employees overcome or otherwise cope with the obstacles they will probably face.

Success Case Evaluation Method

The Success Case Evaluation Method is an impact measurement process that documents the actual performance and business results achieved by trainees in a program. It also pinpoints the performance system factors that enabled, or hindered, training application. The Success Case Evaluation Method is used partially to "prove" the business value of a program, but also—and even more important—to improve it; to accelerate the return on investment (ROI) of training and help build organizational capability to increase business impact from all learning investments.

User Group

The user group comprises licensed and certified users of the Advantage Way system who receive training in the process and have access to the various proprietary tools. The users group networks frequently throughout the year and meets annually at the Advantage Way User Conference.

Bibliography

American Kennel Club. "Bulldog Standard Breed." August 2007. <www.akc.org>.

Brinkerhoff, Robert. *The Success Case Method: Find Out Quickly What's Working and Not*. San Francisco: Berrett-Koehler, 2003.

———. *Telling Training's Story: Evaluation Made Simple, Credible, and Effective*. San Francisco: Berrett-Koehler, 2006.

Brinkerhoff, Robert, and Anne Apking. *High Impact Learning: Strategies for Leveraging Business Results from Training*. New York: Perseus, 2001.

Broad, Mary. *Beyond Transfer of Training: Engaging Systems to Improve Performance*. San Francisco: Pfeiffer, 2005.

International Society for Performance Improvement. "What Is HPT?" September 2007. <www.ispi.org>.

Kirkpatrick, Donald. *Evaluating Training Programs*. New York: McGraw-Hill, 1976.

Kirkpatrick, Donald, and James Kirkpatrick. *Evaluating Training Programs*, Third Edition. San Francisco: Berrett-Koehler, 2006.

Phillips, Jack. *Return on Investment in Training and Performance Improvement Programs*, Second Edition. New York: John Wiley, 2003.

———. "ROI Best Practices." *Chief Learning Officer Magazine* (2003): Available from MediaTec Publishing <www.clomedia.com>.

Robinson, Dana, and James Robinson. *Performance Consulting: Moving Beyond Training*. San Francisco: Berrett-Koehler, 1995.

Rummler, Geary, and Alan Brache. *Improving Performance: How to Manage the White Space on the Organization Chart*. San Francisco: Jossey-Bass, 1995.

Tannenbaum, S., and G. Yukl. "Training and Development in Work Organizations." In *Annual Review of Psychology*, 1992, 43:399–441. Palo Alto, CA: Annual Reviews, Inc.

Wick, Calhoun, Roy Pollock, Andrew Jefferson, and Richard Flanagan. *The Six Disciplines of Breakthrough Learning: How to Turn Training and Development into Business Results*. San Francisco: Pfeiffer, 2006.

Acknowledgments

The inspiration for this book came from the various members of the Advantage Way user group. Their successes, their diligent efforts, and their thoughtful reflections helped us refine the process and showed how important courage was to delivering business results. They are too numerous to name individually but they are represented well by the four individuals who contributed case studies to this book: Lisa Bell, from Holcim; Julie Dervin, from Insight Enterprises; Jeff Hafen, from the Clark County School District; and Larry Mohl, from Children's Healthcare of Atlanta. Thanks also to the past and present officers who work hard to coordinate the users group and help us all benefit from their expertise: Mary Ellen Albritton, Beverly Banks, Dave Basarab, Jeff Hafen, Deanne Jones, and Darell Provencher. We owe them all a debt of gratitude.

We have been fortunate to have longtime business partners in Dennis Dressler, Richard Hodge, and John Hoskins, who have shared the vision and provided leadership to help move the concepts forward. Along the way our colleagues in the Advantage Performance Group (APG) and BTS family—Jonas Akerman, Hayden Constance, Nicole De Falco, Eric Flasck, Steve Gill, Tom Heimsoth, Annika McCrea, Steven Orova, Dan Parisi, Peg Ruppert, Rohit Shyam, Per Stahle, Mary Steiner, Irv Stern, and Jeff Tucker—have embraced the concepts and worked courageously with their own customers to help them achieve great results. And finally our associates Henrik Ekelund, Gerhard Diedericks, Stefan Hellberg, Stina Jonsson, Steffen Kunsch, Jan-Marek Pfau, and Conny Bauer are helping to carry the message to organizations in Europe and Africa.

Index

dialogues with stakeholders,
44–46, 50
getting on table, 41–44

C

capacity utilization, 14
CCSD. *See* Clark County School
District
Center for Leadership, 139,
149–151, *152*
central involvement stratagem,
73–74
champions
receptive to Courageous Training,
217–219
from senior executives, 77, 218
channel partners, 24
Chief Learning Officer (CLO), 140,
148
Children's Healthcare of Atlanta,
134–135
action learning components for,
148–149
Center for Leadership, 139,
149–151, *152*
Community of Practice, 151
evaluations, 149
expectations, 143
feedback, 149
Fortune 100 company, 140
HIL, 144
Leadership Next, 151
learning interventions, 147
learning it forward approach,
148–149, 155
managers, 154
Mohl at, 139–158
operational impact,
157–158
partnering, 143
personal change, 153
personal leadership impact,
156–157
resistance, 154
senior executives, 140–142
system leadership impact, 157
training impact, 150
workshops, 146–147

Clark County School District
(CCSD), 135
Advantage Way system, 163–166,
172, 174
business results, 172
Hafen at, 159–174
HIL, 162, 165, 174
Impact Boosters, 168
Impact Map, 167–168, 170
ISO 9000, 172–173
Line of Sight, 170
managers, 163
partnering, 172
resistance, 167
stakeholders, 169
student/teacher/staff
population, 159–160
Success Case Evaluation Method,
162, 164–165, 171, 173–174
trainees, 171
training initiatives, 168–172
CLO. *See* Chief Learning Officer
coaching tools, 23
collaborations, 20
commitment
from managers, 90, 137
from senior executives, 90
Community of Practice, 151
company autonomy, 24
consensus, 22
consultation, 11
Courageous Training leaders,
2–3. *See also* training leaders
action planning, 31
backbone, 31–32
beginning journey, 215
as bulldogs, 50
as business partners/advisors, 74
change and, 221
clarity of, 34
data collection process, 114
digging beneath results, 104
entire process and, 131
feedback to, 90
as leaders, 117
Line of Sight and, 41
meeting resistance, 81
message of, 126

About the Authors

TIM MOONEY is a Vice President with Advantage Performance Group (APG), a wholly owned subsidiary of BTS Group AB. A seasoned performance consulting expert who specializes in assessment, organizational change, and sales effectiveness, Tim has delivered projects in Germany, France, Great Britain, North America, and South Africa. In his role as the Practice Leader for the Advantage Way, Tim is responsible for developing the practice capabilities, growing the business, and working closely with APG and BTS clients globally to ensure measurable results on all projects.

With more than twenty-five years of corporate sales management and consulting experience, Tim is a frequent speaker and writer on the topic of achieving measurable business impact from training.

Prior to joining Advantage in 2000, he served in a senior management capacity for DDI, where his roles included Vice President of Sales and Marketing for Assessment and Regional Vice President. Tim earned a B.A. degree in Psychology from Butler University in Indianapolis and an M.A. degree in Industrial/Organizational Psychology from the University of Akron. He lives in Glen Ellyn, Illinois, with his wife, Beverly, and daughter, Anne. He can be contacted at tmooney@advantageperformance .com.

ROBERT O. BRINKERHOFF, Ed.D., an internationally recognized expert in evaluation and training effectiveness, has provided consultation to dozens of major companies and organizations in

Australia, Europe, New Zealand, Russia, Saudi Arabia, Singapore, South Africa, and the United States.

Brinkerhoff is an author of numerous books on evaluation and training and has been a keynote speaker and presenter at hundreds of conferences and institutes worldwide. Scores of leading corporations and agencies, from Dell Computer and Ford Motor Company to the World Bank and Central Intelligence Agency, have adopted his methods and tools for training effectiveness and evaluation.

He earned a doctorate at the University of Virginia in program evaluation, where he also coordinated a "street academy" for disadvantaged youth for four years. He is currently a principal consultant and alliance partner with APG and Professor Emeritus at Western Michigan University.

Brinkerhoff's work experience includes a five-year stint as an officer in the U.S. Navy during the Vietnam era, a carpenter, charter-boat mate in the West Indies, grocery salesman in Puerto Rico, and factory laborer in Birmingham, England, where he saw the original Beatles. He has four children, thankfully mostly chronologically grown, and lives with his wife and several unruly dogs in Richland, Michigan. He can be reached at robert .brinkerhoff@wmich.edu.

△ BTS
Catalysts for Profitability and Growth

BTS is an international consulting and learning company that partners with its clients to accelerate change and improve business results. We are a world leader in business simulations and other discovery-based solutions for learning and development initiatives that support companies' efforts for change relating to:

- New strategies and key performance indicators
- Revised business objectives
- Process-efficiency improvements
- Leadership and executive development programs
- Sales effectiveness initiatives
- Merger and acquisition processes

BTS has more than twenty years of experience in delivering business results through innovative methodologies.

With more than 300 professionals located around the world, BTS and its wholly owned subsidiary Advantage Performance Group (APG) serve thirty-five of the world's 100 largest corporations. For more information, please visit

BTS: www.bts.com

APG: www.advantageperformance.com

+1.800.494.6646

242

About Berrett-Koehler Publishers

Berrett-Koehler is an independent publisher dedicated to an ambitious mission: Creating a World That Works for All.

We believe that to truly create a better world, action is needed at all levels—individual, organizational, and societal. At the individual level, our publications help people align their lives with their values and with their aspirations for a better world. At the organizational level, our publications promote progressive leadership and management practices, socially responsible approaches to business, and humane and effective organizations. At the societal level, our publications advance social and economic justice, shared prosperity, sustainability, and new solutions to national and global issues.

A major theme of our publications is "Opening Up New Space." They challenge conventional thinking, introduce new ideas, and foster positive change. Their common quest is changing the underlying beliefs, mind-sets, institutions, and structures that keep generating the same cycles of problems, no matter who our leaders are or what improvement programs we adopt.

We strive to practice what we preach—to operate our publishing company in line with the ideas in our books. At the core of our approach is *stewardship*, which we define as a deep sense of responsibility to administer the company for the benefit of all of our stakeholder groups: authors, customers, employees, investors, service providers, and the communities and environment around us.

We are grateful to the thousands of readers, authors, and other friends of the company who consider themselves to be part of the BK Community. We hope that you, too, will join us in our mission.

Be Connected

VISIT OUR WEB SITE

Go to www.bkconnection.com to read exclusive previews and excerpts of new books, find detailed information on all Berrett-Koehler titles and authors, browse subject-area libraries of books, and get special discounts.

SUBSCRIBE TO OUR FREE E-NEWSLETTER

Be the first to hear about new publications, special discount offers, exclusive articles, news about bestsellers, and more! Get on the list for our free e-newsletter by going to www.bkconnection.com.

GET QUANTITY DISCOUNTS

Berrett-Koehler books are available at quantity discounts for orders of ten or more copies. Please call us toll-free at (800) 929-2929 or E-mail us at bkp.orders@aidcvt.com.

HOST A READING GROUP

For tips on how to form and carry on a book reading group in your workplace or community, see our web site at www.bkconnection.com.

JOIN THE BK COMMUNITY

Thousands of readers of our books have become part of the BK Community by participating in events featuring our authors, reviewing draft manuscripts of forthcoming books, spreading the word about their favorite books, and supporting our publishing program in other ways. If you would like to join the BK Community, please contact us at bkcommunity@bkpub.com.